D1202191

BETHANY
COLLEGE
LIBRARY

THE PALESTINIAN COVENANT
AND ITS MEANING

The Palestinian Covenant and its Meaning

Y. HARKABI

VALLENTINE, MITCHELL

First published 1979 in Great Britain by
VALLENTINE, MITCHELL & CO. LTD.
Gainsborough House, Gainsborough Road,
London, E11 1RS, England

and in the United States of America by
VALLENTINE, MITCHELL & CO. LTD.
c/o Biblio Distribution Centre
81 Adams Drive, P.O. Box 327, Totowa, N.J. 07511

Copyright © 1979 Y. Harkabi

ISBN 0 85303 200 9 (Case)

ISBN 0 85303 201 7 (Paper)

*All rights reserved. No part of this publication may be
reproduced, stored in a retrieval system, or transmitted in any
form or by any means, electronic, mechanical photocopying
recording or otherwise, without the prior permission of
Vallentine, Mitchell & Co. Ltd. in writing.*

Printed and bound in Great Britain by
A. Wheaton & Co. Ltd., Exeter

Contents

322.42
H225p

INTRODUCTION

Introduction

The Palestinian National Covenant is the central document of the Palestinian Liberation Organisation (PLO). It contains the major tenets of its ideology, its main arguments, its strategic objectives and an outline of its programme to achieve these objectives. The ideas succinctly outlined in the Covenant are repeated many times over in Palestinian publications and debates. Thus the Covenant may serve as the best introduction to PLO thinking.

Historically, the Covenant preceded the establishment of the PLO. In some respects the Covenant gave birth to the movement, as it was the blueprint according to which the PLO was established. About three months before the organisation was created in mid-1964, Ahmed Shuqairy[1] formulated and published a draft of the Covenant as a means of introducing the organisation that he planned to set up, to explain its nature to the Palestinians and obtain the consent of the Arab states to its establishment. In his memoirs, Shuqairy recalls: 'Firstly, I started by laying down the Palestinian entity on paper, like the engineer who traces the plan of a building with all its foundations, details and measurements. I wrote, altered, erased and changed the order of the articles until I formulated the "National Covenant" and the "Fundamental Law" of the Palestine Liberation Organisation.[2] I invested all my experience of the Palestinian problem, both on the Arab and international planes, in their composition, taking into consideration the circumstances under which the Palestinian people were living. More than once I spent two or three nights over one single word or phrase, as I was facing generations of Palestinians who read between the lines more

9

than they read the lines themselves' (*From the Summit to Defeat, with the Kings and Presidents* (Arabic) pp. 60–61).[3] Borrowing ideas from previous discussions on the activation of a Palestinian political movement, Shuqairy, no doubt, demonstrated great skill in summarising and moulding them as ideological tenets in a full-fledged Covenant.

The PLO Constituent Congress which Shuqairy convened in East Jerusalem introduced few changes in Shuqairy's draft and approved it on 2 June 1964. It thus became the first version of the Covenant (see Appendix A).

Man is an ideological animal. Taking action he meditates, plans, rationalises, justifies and gives sense to his behaviour. The same applies to social and political collectivities. Ideology is a sort of *dialogue* such collectivities conduct with themselves before, during and after action. Ideology is required for any political movement as the means of producing its specific communality, expounding to its members the objectives it sets out to accomplish, its attitudes, historical perspectives and pro-grammes of action. A political movement may canonize its ideology in documents so as to communicate its ideas and serve as a guide to its followers. The PLO's Covenant is such an example. Basically it is the dialogue of the PLO with itself.

The nature of the Palestinian Covenant was influenced by the circumstances in which the PLO was established. Divergent conceptions prevailed among the Palestinians on the question of their role in the conflict and their organisation; this was due to their dispersion and their ideological affiliations in the differ-ent Arab host countries. Arab governments were suspicious of the plan to organise the Palestinians into what was then commonly called 'the Palestinian entity'. Hence the Covenant had to be formulated both to satisfy the different currents of opinion among the Palestinians and allay the suspicions of the Arab governments. Its text then had to be codified and enshrined in a document which although merely a platform or a summation of political views, was elevated to the lofty status generally accorded to constitutions, as regards its authority and the difficulty of amending it. It was designed to be the framework of basic guidelines for PLO activities.

Furthermore, as a common denominator the Covenant fulfils a function in assuring the ideological cohesion of the Palestinian movement. The importance of this role increased in the post-Shuqairy period as the Fedayeen organisations became the major components of the PLO, and the PLO changed its nature and composition from basically individual to corporate membership of the Fedayeen groups and their affiliates. In such circumstances the danger of dissension became more acute, entailing a potential split and the desertion of a whole group. The Covenant thus serves as a doctrinal bond that ties together all the subgroups of the PLO. It is, therefore, not accidental that declarations of allegiance to the Covenant in PLO documents are more frequent in the post-Shuqairy period and in particular in recent years; the resolutions of the 'Palestinian National Councils' (PNCs)[4] usually start with reverential references to the Covenant (see preambles of the resolutions of the 12th and 13th PNCs in Appendices E and F). The greater the danger of internal discord, the greater the need to cling to the Covenant.

Precisely because of the cohesive role the Covenant fulfils, it is difficult to amend it, since change may seriously affect the entire organisation. Only if a consensus is reached can a change be made without jeopardising the coherence of the organisation. Thus the Covenant has been amended only once—in the 4th PNC in July 1968—in order to meet the demands and views of the Fedayeen groups which were participating for the first time in the PNC, as the centre of gravity of the PLO moved towards them. Since then, despite many opportunities, up to the last—the 13th PNC—ten PNCs (including an extraordinary one) have been convened and the Covenant has not been amended. It is not clear whether there are circles in the PLO who would have liked to amend it. The PLO is not only a political movement possessing a Covenant, but is straitjacketed by it as well.

The Palestinian Covenant declares as its central tenet a total repudiation of the existence of Israel, and institutionalises this stand and the theoretical and practical implications that derive from it in an ideological system. The claim that Israel should not exist is implied in almost half of its thirty-three articles, including those that are formulated as definitions and axioms. By definition, the demand for the demise of Israel becomes a matter of an inevitable necessity, a kind of scientific truth. Israel must cease to exist not so much because the Palestinians have an interest in her disappearance, but because this disappearance is derived from the definition of Palestinism as the attribute of both a people and a country. Palestine is the homeland of the Palestinians and must not be separated from the Arab world; and the Palestinians are an integral part of the Arab nation. The *whole* of Palestine must be restored to them and put under their sovereignty, because only in Palestine in its entirety could they realise their self-determination, redeem their personality from alienation and regain their dignity and freedom. This conception is complemented by the theory, that is also formulated as a definition, that the Jews are not a nation and thus on principle do not deserve to have a state of their own, nor can they as a non-nation maintain it. Precisely because Israel contradicts such axioms both in regard to the territory she has occupied and the essence of the Israeli Jews, it is concluded that its establishment could only have been accomplished in an historical act of aggression and plunder by a despicable movement such as Zionism. Zionism is condemned both because it is racist and linked with imperialism and because its evil deeds flow from its very essence. The abolition of Israel's existence is legal and also beneficial to humanity, the Arabs and the Palestinians. The Covenant thus encompasses intrinsic, moral, utilitarian, volitional, legal and historical arguments, which all converge into a total negation, as a matter of principle, of the existence of the State of Israel in any form or size.[5] The plethora of arguments in the Covenant as to why Israel should not exist may perhaps have a cumulative effect, impelling the PLO leaders and their public to believe that there is no atrocity that cannot be justified in order to bring about the liquidation of Israel.

One must be cautious and restrained in assessing national movements and their doctrines, especially when they are at loggerheads with one's own. However, I cannot help feeling that the Covenant is an ugly document according to its stand. It is not a manifesto of an extreme, lunatic fringe faction, but the essence of the outlook of the centre and mainstream of the Palestinian movement. The Covenant represents an egoistic stand that does not show the slightest consideration for the adversary, nor any trace of recognition that he too may have a grievance, a claim and justice. The Palestinian movement claims absoluteness and 'totality'—there is absolute justice in the Palestinian stand in contrast to the absolute injustice of Israel;

an unqualified Manichaean division of good and evil; right is on the Palestinian side only; only they are worthy of self-determination; the Israelis are barely human creatures who at most may be tolerated in the Palestinian state as individuals or as a religious community, with their numbers reduced to 5 per cent of their present level (Article 6 in the 1968 version) and then assimilated in an Arab environment; the historical link of the Jews with the land of Israel is deceit; the spiritual link as expressed in the centrality of the land of Israel in Judaism is a fraud; international decisions such as the Mandate granted by the League of Nations and the United Nations Partitions Resolution are all consigned to nothingness in a cavalier manner.

The Covenant, from beginning to end, in every one of its articles, is characterised by one-sidedness; the Palestinians arrogate rights that they are not prepared to grant to their rivals. There is no ray of light in Zionism; it is totally depraved. History is distorted—Zionism is represented as if it were from the start a conquering movement, while in fact its achievements were brought about by hard labour and its lands bought with money, and a case can be made that the Arabs by their attacks on Israel forced it into conquests. As against the vices of Zionism, Palestinians bathe in self-righteousness, conferring on themselves spiritual virtues and moral values. The Covenant is a document of arrogance, without a sign of the humility that should be the lot of the human condition; it is completely expressed in absolute terms, without traces of any relativity.

The Covenant provides an example of the mischief of absolute national ideologies and the need for relativity in political positions in general, and more so, in conflict situations. It is a lesson we should all learn. Absolutist political positions as in the Covenant should be rejected whatever their provenance.[6]

Relativism follows from recognition that the adversary, too, has rights and aspirations, is also enmeshed in contradictions, dilemmas of his human existence, and writhes in their agony and that he, too, possesses a moral personality. A relativist position is an extension of the Kantian categorical imperative—in a conflict situation—to view the adversary as constituting a moral agent and a goal, not merely a target to hit.

A relativist position is required even in a practical manner as a precept of conventional wisdom that political entities do not act in the world in isolation and that an extreme position taken by one side, or a far-reaching action, may be considered by his rivals a provocation and a transgression to which he may over-react in a fashion detrimental to both sides. Hence, the need for individuals, as well as for nations, to behave prudently, exercise restraint, and endeavour to search for conciliation and compromise.

Such an approach is a head on negation of the PLO position. For the PLO a compromise is anathema. A conciliatory attitude was denigrated as a despicable 'compromising mentality' by the 11th PNC (see commentary to Article 21 and Appendix D).

The basic ideology of the PLO is totalistic in the sense that it insists on achieving its goal in its entirety. The PLO polarises and impoverishes the choice as if only two possibilities exist: the liquidation of Israel or the liquidation of the Palestinian problem as a collective death sentence on the Palestinians as a people. This approach rules out a compromise as a partial achievement of goals. According to the PLO definition any agreement to the existence of Israel, even in limited dimensions, constitutes a total defeat for the Palestinians and their national ruin.

The conflict is presented as a zero-game and a deadly quarrel of survival without compromise. We say 'yes' to Palestine, the Palestinian state, and therefore we say 'no' to Israel. Saying 'yes' both to Palestine and to Israel is proscribed. One may, and perhaps even should, agree that the Palestinians have justified grievances; one may have sympathy for their suffering. In my view, it should be recognised that their group identity should be given concrete political expression, but the solution that stems from their ideology must be rejected with the utmost reprobation.

The Covenant could have served Israel in the struggle against Arab positions in the international arena. Arab attitudes have grappled with the difficulty of publicly brandishing the explicit goal of the liquidation of Israel. The formulation of national policy in modern times requires consideration of the need to mobilise the support of foreign governments and public opinion. This need is acute for small states, for in order for their external policies to be effective they have to convince the big nations and gain their political and material support. The Arabs have been aware of this. Throughout the conflict Arab spokesmen have toiled to clothe the aim of Israel's liquidation in the garments of positive formulae: 'the liberation of Palestine'; 'return'; 'realisation of self-determination for the Palestinians'; 'á just solution'; 'the establishment of a democratic state', etc. In these phrases, there is a tendency to avoid saying explicitly that realisation of the goal involves the liquidation of Israel as a political entity, i.e., to talk in a positive fashion about the achievements they seek to accomplish, ignoring their by-products. Arab and Palestinian spokesmen disclaim the intention to 'destroy' Israel. Indeed they probably hope that its physical assets—buildings, industry etc.—will stay after their conquest of it. However, this is only a quibble; the destruction of Israel means its liquidation as a political entity.

Despite its blatant anti-Israeli content, the Palestinian Covenant does not contain the expression 'liquidation of Israel' (the nearest expressions are: the 'elimination of Zionism in Palestine' (Article 15); 'entire illegality of the establishment of Israel' (Article 19); and 'destroy the Zionist presence' (Article 22)). In their dispute with Israel the Arabs have spoken in algebraic terms, whose meaning has been the liquidation of Israel, without always spelling it out. After 1967, there has developed in the principal Arab circles a trend to present Israel with supposedly reasonable demands and formulate a political plan of action that would appear feasible and just: the aim was to demonstrate a pragmatic approach and give an impression of moderation, while glossing over the situation that would result from the fulfilment of these demands, and which would bring closer the possibility of achieving the old goal—the abolition of Israel's existence. Israel's refusal to abide by these demands has been presented as intransigence which was perpetuating the dispute. In a sophisticated move of this kind the Arabs have aspired to win over public opinion from recognition of the legitimacy of their demands and their plan of action to a recognition, even tacit, of the legitimacy of their final goal, which could remain extremist. They have combined tactical flexibility with strategic rigidity, while putting off the discussion of their long-term aims, or the situation that would transpire with the fulfilment of their demands. In this way, they have also endeavoured to turn Israel into a guilty defendant while evading commitments to end the conflict in a situation of permanent coexistence. In the Palestinian arenas, the Arabs emphatically demand national self-determination for the Palestinians, playing down the latent significance in the fulfilment of this demand for Israel according to the conception of the PLO, whom the Arab states have authorised to formulate the Palestinian claims. This self-determination involves the right to define the destiny of the whole of Palestine by establishing an Arab nation-state over the entire territory while abrogating the Israelis' right to self-determination and the right to have a Jewish state.

The magic formula uttered by commentators that Arab extremism is merely a display of emotionalism that should not be taken at its face value does not apply with regard to a meticulously drafted and polished doctrinal document such as the Palestinian Covenant. The rejection of Israel in the Covenant is not an emotional outburst or a rhetorical expedient, but a contrived political conception, a carefully worked out doctrine, and a well-built ideology. It is not hatred but reasoned hostility, on the cognitive and not just affective level. The Covenant is the soul of the PLO and the PLO is still today the central factor of the Palestinian camp. A declaration of the leaders in the West Bank that the PLO represents them means that the Covenant, with all its absolutist implications, is their guiding light. This applies to the Israeli Arabs who identify with the PLO. Arab states' support of the PLO which reached its climax in the Algiers and Rabat summit meetings in which they officially undertook to follow the line of policy as formulated by the PLO (see commentary to Article 29) means signing a blank check for PLO extremism. The Arab states cannot disclaim responsibility for the PLO absolutism which they have most authoritatively endorsed.

As circumstances change an ideological document may pass from its inspirational and operational phase in which it influences the thinking and behaviour of its followers to its ritualisation—a phase of vacuous verbalisation of its ideas, and then to its demise, as its ideas are discarded first partially and then completely. However, the dynamics of this depletion of a document's ideological vigor and influence varies in speed and thoroughness.

One may be struck by the persistence of the extraordinary centrality of the Palestinian Covenant as the main depository of PLO ideology in the Palestinian movement. This persistence can be documented by the continuing salience of its ideas in Palestinian political thinking. The Covenant is not the handiwork of a past generation, which, as its irrelevancy transpires, the present generation may consider an onerous burden to be rid of, as some people allege is the case as regards Marxism in the USSR. The Covenant is the handiwork of the present generation.

The PLO is of course alive to the difficulty of converting the ideas of the Covenant into reality. Yet the contradictions between the exigency of the hour and PLO ideology do not necessarily undermine its hold on its followers, for its realisation may be put off to a later stage. Thus the PLO ideology is saved from attrition by the dire facts of reality, by the conviction of many Arabs and Palestinians that the basic disparity between them and Israel in manpower, resources and political stature, etc., ultimately promises a victory to the Arab side. It is precisely these circumstances which endow the Covenant and the Palestinian and Arab positions in the conflict with a considerable longevity.

Despite its paramount importance the Covenant does not decree eternity on the Arab-Israeli conflict or finality on the Palestinian position. The Covenant is not a litany which the Palestinians recite daily. No doubt, many ordinary Palestinians are not very acquainted with its details. Like any ideological document, the Covenant does not necessarily dictate every step the PLO takes, although it lays down the political direction of the PLO and the general orientation of its movement. Peoples may attain political settlements in spite of sacrosanct conceptions. No national document or doctrine can be regarded as a fetter that cannot be broken. The pressure of facts may in the last resort lead the Palestinians to turn their backs on the Covenant. A settlement may begin on the political-diplomatic level but it should percolate through to the national ideology and affect the climate of opinion. A political settlement that does not bring a change in national positions, such as those expressed in the Covenant, may not last long. Thus, as long as the Covenant is in force, it makes a real settlement with the Palestinians extremely difficult to achieve. Palestinian circles who oppose the settlement will use the Covenant, if it remains valid, to gore their more moderate opponents. It is no coincidence that the 'Popular

Front' of Dr Habash relies on the Covenant in its argument against the participation of the Palestinians in a Geneva conference.

The full significance and difficulty of a change in the stand of the PLO, for instance, in the form of recognition of Israel's right to exist, must be fully appreciated. It is easy for a political movement to alter a marginal concept in its basic stand, but a national movement will find it difficult to change the *core value* in its system of beliefs—in the case of the PLO—that the *whole* of Palestine is the homeland of the Palestinians and should be returned to them.

The absolutist and totalistic tenor of the PLO's ideology is deeply ingrained in its whole outlook. Consent to coexist with Israel is a head-on clash with its beliefs. Thus a change means a momentous transvaluation, not a change *in* its outlook, but *of* its outlook in its entirety, touching the most profound chords of the PLO ethos—from PLO to PPLO ('Part of Palestine Liberation Organisation').

There is also a structural difficulty in changing the Covenant. The Covenant constitutes a cohesive unity and in many of its articles the absolutist stand on removing Israel is implied. Hence it is impossible to amend one or few articles, leaving the rest intact. Adjusting the Covenant to the idea of coexistence with Israel necessitates the forsaking of the whole Covenant or rewriting it from beginning to end. Furthermore, the nature of the Covenant and the Palestinian position exclude the possibility of a gradual piecemeal incremental change which is usually easier to achieve than a once-and-for-all complete change.

PLO leaders labour under grave constitutional constraints. Shuqairy as chairman of the PLO Executive Committee (the Cabinet managing the daily affairs of the PLO), despite the lively opposition to his personal leadership, had much greater power in the PLO than Yasser Arafat. Administratively, Shuqairy appointed the members of the Executive Committee, whereas after the changes introduced by the fourth PNC in the PLO Constitution (or its Fundamental Law) the PNC has elected the Executive Committee members who, in their turn, appoint their chairman, and in this fashion Arafat has been appointed and reappointed in subsequent PNCs to his present post. Shuqairy had greater latitude in making statements on the PLO position and in some instances surprised the members of the Executive Committee. Actually they had no constituency of their own and most of them were dependent on Shuqairy.

Since the 4th PNC the PLO has been based on corporate membership of the Fedayeen organisations, and its leadership has become a collective one. Executive Committee members are delegates of their organisations and Arafat has to look constantly over his shoulder and must watch the reaction of his colleagues in the Executive Committee to the smallest move he makes.

Furthermore, constitutionally only a PNC is entitled to pronounce judgment on basic issues or moderate positions. Between PNCs the PLO is paralysed with regard to the possibility of changing a substantial position; PLO leaders may at most express their personal views, which does not commit the PLO. It may be that some individuals, even in the higher echelons of the PLO, have indeed moderated their private views, a development which can be hailed and welcomed if one could substantiate it and specify its details, but it is irrelevant as far as the corporate position of the PLO is concerned so long as a PNC has not followed suit.

In recent years journalists have repeatedly found it difficult to accommodate themselves to these limiting factors and have announced that in a very special interview they had with a PLO dignitary the ice had been broken and that there had been a change in the PLO position. The psychological temptation of journalists to pose as the midwives of history, by whose efforts a new period will be ushered in, is very understandable. Such scoops may serve the self-esteem of the journalist but do no service to the truth. It should be instructive that all such good tidings have come to naught. In some cases a denial was issued the next day by the person interviewed, stating that he had been misunderstood, and in other cases such a denial was published by one of the PLO offices.

There is one lesson to be learned from this oft-repeated story of false hopes of change—only from the august site of a PNC can a change in position be announced. To make sure that there will be no deviation from this rule, the 12th PNC clearly prescribed that the leadership of the PLO (its Executive Committee) would occupy itself only with tactics: 'In the light of this programme [the political programme enacted by the PNC, Y.H.]

the leadership of the revolution will determine the tactics which will serve as and make possible the realization of these objectives . . . should a situation arise harmful to the destiny and the future of the Palestinian people, the National Assembly, i.e.. PNC will be convened in extraordinary session' (see Appendix E).

Indeed the predicament of the PLO, the internal and external pressures its leaders have to cope with, their anxiety that the PLO may be left out of the negotiations, their foreboding about their basic contradiction with Jordan, all these have to be appreciated to understand their behaviour. Because of the pressures they encounter, they have developed a knack for verbal ploys to escape embarrassing situations. Thus, one has to distinguish carefully between what formula or phrase constitutes a real change in PLO's position and what is only a *pseudo-change* or pseudo-moderation. For instance, the announcement of PLO readiness to accept a state on the West Bank was presented by PLO spokesmen and hailed by its sympathisers as a momentous change and some even explained that such a state hides somewhere in its profundities an incipient readiness to recognise Israel. That this is not the case is attested by the resolutions of the 12th and 13th PNCs (see commentaries to Article 21). Acceptance of such a state was stipulated as a part of an incremental process aimed at Israel's demise and buttressed by the explicit condition that the acceptance does not involve recognition of peace and secure borders. The same applies to the PLO's expression of readiness, or rather demand, to participate in the Geneva negotiations; this does not imply recognition of Israel or readiness for permanent coexistence with Israel. A straightforward proof to this effect is that the PLO demands that its participation be based on the General Assembly Resolution 3236 and not on the Security Council Resolution 242 (see Article 21). The contention frequently put forward by PLO advocates that the PLO reserves recognition of Israel as a last card in the negotiations is simply dishonest. They claim that PLO non-recognition so far is only a gambit and an opening stratagem. The PLO plays on people's credulity, pleading that recognition is their only, ultimate concession, held in reserve for the final showdown. This is not the case. A bargaining card is something the partner is eager to have and ready to pay for. Nothing helps Israel vis-à-vis the PLO more than the latter's persistent refusal to recognise Israel's right to exist and thus its tacit admission of destructive intentions. It is in fact the Palestinians who need to recognise Israel's right to exist in order to pave the way for their own international recognition and participation in the negotiations. Non-recognition of Israel is the core value or central doctrine in the PLO creed and strategy, and to claim that it is only an innocent tactical bargaining card is a grotesque absurdity. One could as well assume that communism is the Soviet bargaining card which its leaders intend to concede at the successful end of the SALT negotiations.

A trenchant proof that the PLO has moderated its position has been produced by alluding to PFLP accusations against the PLO mainstream that PLO readiness to participate in a Geneva conference is a betrayal of the Arab and Palestinian cause. Thus salvation comes from unexpected quarters—the testimony of the most extreme. However, such reasoning is defective. Mutual accusations of betrayal have been very common in inter-Arab relations. There is nothing to signify that Arafat's enmity toward Israel is less than that of the PFLP leader Dr Habash. The squabble between the different PLO factions is mainly concerned with problems of tactics. On the basic non-acceptance of Israel there has always been a consensus. Furthermore, significantly, most delegates of the so-called Rejection Front joined the mainstream of the PLO on the political resolutions of the 13th PNC.[7]

So far there is no indication to the present time that a PNC is ready to moderate the PLO position. As the convening of the 13th PNC approached, many prognostications were offered that the big hour was approaching and the PNC would modify the PLO position and even amend the Covenant. These prophecies all proved to be misguided; even Article 6 in the Covenant, the amendment of which would have been much easier, was not attempted (see commentary to Article 6). Had there been the smallest inclination to change the PLO's position, the 13th Council could have refrained in its resolution from declaring allegiance to the Covenant, as a first step in the direction of extricating itself from the embrace of the Covenant, by a process of consigning it to oblivion. This would have been a convenient alternative to a straightforward abrogation. The recurring reverential references in this PNC's resolutions are ominous in indicating that not only is the PLO not changing its position but that it does not even intend to change.

History should not be straitjacketed in logical speculations. Let us suppose that harassed by Arab pressures, haunted by its anxieties, lured by the promised dialogue with the US, an institution like the Central Council[8] may one day express some readiness to accept Resolution 242. It would be foolhardy to exclude such an eventuality even if it entailed a split in the PLO. However, the question will arise as to what reservations or qualifications would be appended to such an acceptance. For instance, the PLO leadership, or part of it, may hedge such an acceptance with the provision that the national rights of the Palestinians, their national self-determination or their right to return to their homeland be recognised or assured.

The problem that will then be posed is that for the PLO such provisions may serve as a verbal means to empty the acceptance of 242 or the recognition of Israel of binding content. For in PLO parlance Palestinian national rights or their self-determination is the right to the entire country (see Article 19), and the right to return means the right to subvert Israel by an influx of Palestinians to whom their 'homes' would be returned with the Israelis being evicted (see commentary to Article 6—The Democratic State). Thus, such reservation may forfeit the acceptance of 242 altogether.

PLO verbal niceties may appear to the foreign observer who is not acquainted with the tenor of the debates in the PLO as outlandish sophistry; it is dire reality in the Middle East. Changing a position involves an internal alteration in the subject's cognition. That is why it is so important to understand the ways he thinks on the issue, and the specific connotation of his vocabulary for himself, thus, to examine semantically the language the PLO uses.

What is then the test to see whether the PLO has moderated its views and relativised its absolutist position? My answer is— if the PLO recognises that the Palestinian national right to self-determination applies to only *part* of Palestine, thus becoming a PPLO (Part of Palestine Liberation Organisation) and if this recognition is accompanied by a statement of readiness to terminate the conflict and live henceforth in peace with Israel. Such a change has to be most explicit, for concealing it in vague expressions implies that it is a defective recognition from which it may try to release itself at the earliest opportunity.

No doubt, it is not easy for the PLO to make such a change. Without it we are marking time. The PLO has been to such great lengths in its negation of Israel that the way back is not easy or short. The acknowledgement of a change, in order to be effective, has to have considerable substance to counterbalance the accumulated weight of the PLO's rejection of Israel, or to undo the dominance of the absolutist destructive position that has become so deeply ingrained in the Arab ethos.

At the moment there are no clear indications of readiness to make such a change.

Any analysis of contemporary politics is in the nature of a 'progress report' as an account of what has occurred so far. The rate of obsolescence in political writing is extremely high. I only hope that the validity of my analysis of the PLO position expires soon, and I would be only too delighted to report it. Still, I have to describe what I see and not what I *hope* to see. It is only self-deception to describe the past and the present in the terms of developments hoped for in the future, in our case to report that the PLO has moderated its position because we hope to see such a change come true. Attributing to the present time an expected quality does not signify far-sightedness but myopia; it stops being a politically realistic approach and becomes a self-indulgent fantasy.

A methodological observation is worth making. The methodology followed in the commentaries to the articles of the Covenant is a close examination of their literal meaning. Such an approach is *prima facie* open to the criticism of 'misplaced literalism', attributing to phrases a rigorous literal meaning which was not in the mind of those who uttered or wrote them, who may have expressed them in a cavalier, figurative or rhetorical fashion; and it may be claimed that the analysis should be political rather than literal.

Such a contention seems to me to be erroneous. The PLO is not carefree in the use of words; its resolutions are debated fiercely and attention is given to every phrase. If words are important for the PLO, so is their meaning. We do not possess X-rays to penetrate the souls of PLO leaders and examine their inner thoughts. We can only examine their attitude or positions by their words and action. PLO resolutions serve as a means by which its leaders announce their position to their audience. If such resolutions are assumed to have been phrased as demagogy to achieve popularity in the Palestinian and Arab public, then at least one can conclude that the resolutions attest to what ideas the leaders think are popular or potentially so; only by manipulating a popular symbol can one achieve popularity and consent. If this assumption is correct, the PLO resolutions reveal the current views of Arab public opinion. It seems more reasonable to assume that PLO resolutions are means by which the leaders propagate their ideas, and as such they testify what the views of the leadership are, or what views they want the public to attribute to them; even as such, they are significant.

The behaviour of the PLO has not contradicted its words, but on the contrary has supported them. Action may have fallen short of what was described or reflected by words, but that does not at all indicate bad faith but human frailty and the usual gap between desires and accomplishments.

An explanation of PLO views which is not based on the analysis of their meaning may err in attributing to the PLO political positions which the PLO did not entertain. Such a tendency, not to project PLO thinking but rather to mould it for the PLO, has been quite common among some Israeli and foreign commentators. Let us pay attention to PLO pronouncements. Brushing them aside, even with the best intentions, such as a desire to avoid seeing their unpleasant aspects. unwittingly implies contempt towards the PLO.

My first commentaries on the Palestinian Covenant were published in English in the *New York University Journal of International Law and Politics*, Vol. 3, No. 1, Spring 1970. This essay drew the attention of the public to the Covenant for the first time. These new commentaries are more detailed and their scope has been widened to explore how the conceptions of the PLO have evolved against the background of the Covenant. I have used the commentaries to explain some major aspects of the Palestinian and Arab positions in the conflict, so as to outline a general summary of these positions for readers who are interested in the intricacies of this tragic conflict.

ANALYSIS
OF THE
PALESTINIAN NATIONAL
COVENANT

The Palestinian National Covenant (1968)

This Covenant will be called the 'Palestinian National Covenant'
(*al-mīthāq al-watanī al-filastīnī*).

Mīthāq means Covenant as an agreement of binding significance.
The word appears in this sense in the Koran. In the PLO's
official English translation of the 1964 original document *mīthāq*
was rendered into English as 'Covenant', while in the translation
of the 1968 version as 'Charter'. Thus 'Covenant' or 'Charter'
are equally correct. It should be noted that documents such as
the League of Nations' Charter, the UN Charter and the Arab
League Charter are also called *mīthāq* in Arabic. The resolutions
passed at Palestinian congresses during the Mandate since 1919
were also called *mīthāq qawmī*. A less ceremonious use of the
word *mīthāq* is that of an ideological platform of a party, or
'manifesto'.

The Covenant or Charter is the basic document of the PLO
summing up the organisation's attitudes and policy. In the
regulations of the 'Popular Organisation' of the PLO, Article 5
lays down: 'Active membership of the Palestine Liberation
Organisation is open to every Arab Palestinian, male or female,
on condition that he is registered with the Organisation and
undertakes to adhere to the Covenant'. Article 9 repeats this
regulation (*'the Constitution of the Popular Palestinian
Organisation'* in the official PLO pamphlet on the second
Palestine National Council (PNC), or in *Documents on
Palestine 1965*, pp. 297–8). The commitment to adhere to the
Covenant has been reaffirmed in Palestinian declarations and
resolutions of the Palestinian National Councils.

In the Covenant promulgated in 1964, the adjective 'national'
was rendered by *qawmī*, whereas in the 1968 version it was
changed to *watanī*. (*Watanī* had been originally used in

27

Shuqairy's draft of the Covenant and from this viewpoint the amended version of 1968 is a return to the draft.) In present-day Arabic *qawmī* means 'national' in the sense of pan-Arab, ethnic nationalism. *Watanī* on the other hand, means national in its limited sense, in its narrow, territorial framework, i.e., patriotism of a specific Arab country (see below, commentary to Article 1). It should also be noted that the Egyptian National Charter of 1962 was called *al-Mīthāq al-Watanī*.

Presumably the use of the adjective *qawmī* in 1964 was meant to stress the bond of the Palestinians with pan-Arabism, which was due to the PLO's insecurity when it was founded, and its need to assert that it would adjust itself to the policy of the Arab states. The change in 1968, on the other hand, stressed Palestinian patriotism and the independence of the Palestinian movement as elaborated in Fatah doctrines (see Article 28).

ARTICLES OF THE COVENANT[9]

Article 1
Palestine is the homeland of the Arab Palestinian people: it is an indivisible part of the Arab homeland, and the Palestinian people are an integral part of the Arab nation.

The version in the 1964 Covenant was vaguer: 'Palestine is an Arab homeland bound by strong Arab national ties to the rest of the Arab countries, which together form the great Arab homeland.' In the spirit of the trend of stressing Palestinism, the amended version of the Covenant presents the country not as an Arab homeland but specifically as the homeland of the Palestinian Arab people.

The phrase 'the Palestinian Arab people' recurs in the Covenant as the official nomenclature of the Palestinians as a political collectivity. In previous documents, including many of Nasser's speeches, the Palestinians are called *ahl filastin*—men of Palestine. This expression has become rare recently as the recognition of them as a political community took root. The use of another term of a similar meaning 'Palestinian entity' (*kiyān filastin*) has too become rarer in recent years. It reappeared in the 12th PNC apparently in order to get round the need for calling the Palestinian state in the West Bank by the name of 'state', because according to the PLO's view such a state would not be a consummate state but only a stage to be followed by expansion to the whole territory of Palestine. Conversely, the use of the term 'entity' is frequent as regards Israel, which as a substitute for its usual name is described as the 'Zionist entity.'

The definition that 'Palestine is the homeland of the Palestinian Arab people' may give the impression that the existence of the Palestinian people is an incontestable historical fact, and as if Palestine has always been the homeland of such a people. This glosses over the need to discuss the problem of the historicity of the Palestinian people.

Apart from the Israeli period, 'Palestine' has never been a political unit, in which a unique nationality could emerge. Palestine was a geographical term, not a political one. Previously, an Arab who lived in geographical Palestine tended to describe himself as a Moslem, as an Arab, an Ottoman or as a native of his home town or village. 'Palestine' as a political unit was carved out by the British. 'A Palestinian' in the period of the British Mandate until 1948 meant a person who bore Palestinian citizenship. During the Mandate period, the population of the country was divided into 'Palestinian Jews' and 'Palestinian Arabs.'[10] Similarly, in the UN Partition Resolution of 29 November 1947 Palestine was divided into 'a Jewish state' and 'an Arab state,' and it dawned on nobody to call the latter a Palestinian state. The identification of Jews in Palestine as 'Israelis' left the adjective 'Palestinian' free so that the Palestinian Arabs could acquire it for themselves exclusively.

Thus, this term that expressed nationality or citizenship developed into a national definition for a group of Arabs, who either lived in Palestine or originated from it and became a self-conscious collectivity by the events they lived through in recent decades, though the name Palestine is an ancient one and originates from the Philistines; living on islands in the Mediterranean Sea, who invaded and settled in the southern coastal plain. However, the Palestinian Arabs are not descended from them racially, nor do they derive any inspiration from them culturally.

This first article of the Covenant is the chief article in it and is the essence of the doctrine of Palestinian nationalism. It was placed at the beginning of the Covenant deliberately. It contains a definition of essence and is not an historical narration.

Palestine, as its name says, is by definition the homeland of the Palestinians and it is also a part of the Arab homeland. The point this article intends to drive home is that Palestine was and will remain such a homeland. It is therefore a descriptive analytical sentence, which from the PLO's point of view has presumably normative validity.

In most Arab constitutions the political connection between the specific Arab state and the entire Arab nation of which it forms part is stated, but here this link is reinforced as a dual connection on both the *ethnic* and *territorial* levels.

This article presents three connections or links:

1. A connection between *a people and its country*, i.e., between the Palestinian people and Palestine as its homeland. This connection stems as it were in an axiomatic fashion from semantics: as the country and the people bear an identical name they mutually belong to one another. Palestine belongs to the Palestinian people as a logical imperative. Thus such a connection in the PLO's outlook excludes the possibility that Palestine could also be the homeland of another nationality— the Israeli Jews.

2. A territorial connection between *the territory of Palestine and the Arab homeland*. This connection too receives a great deal of emphasis. It is described as an inseparable tie. The existence of Israel as an independent national unit cuts it off from the Arab homeland and violates this indivisibility. Therefore, it contradicts this axiomatic definition and is consequently rejected. Israel thus cannot exist, too, due to the territorial merger between Palestine and the Arab world.

3. An ethnic connection between the *Palestinian people and the Arab nation* which stems from the fact that the former is a part of the latter.

These connections are presented as indisputable facts of past and present reality and not as goals that should be realised. Their validity is presented as analytical and not normative. The need to grant political expression to these connections derives from their being a factual truth. These connections thus generate the rights of the Palestinians over all of their homeland, such as the right of all of them to return to it (*'awda*) and the right of political self-determination as to the fate of the entire territory.

It should be noted that the dual connections, the ethnic connection of the Palestinians with the Arab nation and the geographical connection of Palestine with the Arab homeland, are not equally binding. (The PLO would vehemently oppose such an analysis.) The Palestinians are linked to the Arab nation by such factors as language, religion, culture and history. If the Palestinians define themselves as part of the Arab nation and are so regarded by the rest of the Arabs, one cannot dispute that. However, as for the territorial connection according to which a plot of land called Palestine is an integral part of the Arab world as if sub specie aeternitatis—such an attachment, even if it existed during the past few hundred years, since Palestine was part of the Ottoman Empire, was a matter of a political arrangement as all borders and states are and not the outcome of an essential affinity.

The concept put forward in this article is associated with the distinction between two types of homeland (*al-watan al-khās*) of the people (*sha'b*) and the great homeland of the Arab nation (*al-watan al-'aām* or *al-watan al-kabīr*). The Arab 'nation' (*umma*) is made up of 'peoples' (*shu'ūb*) and the Arab homeland comprises the national homelands of these peoples. The relationship of the individual Arab to the special homeland and to their people is called *wataniyya* (patriotism) while the relationship of the people and the individual to the overall Arab homeland and nation is called in modern Arabic *qawmiyya* (nationalism). The *qawmiyya* is a wide term, somewhat like the trunk of a tree that branches off into offshoots of local patriotism—*wataniyya*. These distinctions which have spread were developed by the ideologist Satī' al-Ḥusrī: 'And as for the Egyptians, the Iraqis . . . they are nothing but the peoples and branches of one nation, the Arab nation.' (*Arabism First*, p. 13).

The two concepts *qawmiyya* and *wataniyya* are not on the same footing; the fundamental, lasting, basic and complete manifestation in the 'classic' conception of Arab nationalism is *qawmiyya*, while *wataniyya* is presented as something truncated and even transient, as a result of the splitting up of the Arab region into separate states carved out by the colonial powers. However, once Arab unity is achieved and the frontiers wiped out, or at least change their nature and become a kind of demarcation line between districts, *wataniyya* will fade away and *qawmiyya* will hold sole sway. *Qawmiyya* is generally represented as the manifestation of unreserved good, while excessive *wataniyya* is represented as adherence to narrow, local or provincial patriotism, which exists at the expense of pan-Arab nationalism. Generally, terms of opprobrium frequently qualify *wataniyya* such as *iqlimiyya* (regionalism), *qutriyya* (territorialism) and *kiyaniyya* (a derisive term used by Arab radicals condemning the emphasis on Palestinian entity at the expense of Arabism).[11]

This hierarchy, which gives priority to *qawmiyya* over *wataniyya* actually refers more to the ideal of Arab nationalism than the reality, because it can be assumed that the tie of a particular population to its ethnic framework—the family, the tribe, the geographical or political formation or the individual's link and identification with his neighbourhood and human environment are generally stronger than any bond with pan-Arabism. There are also grounds for assuming that the crystallisation and perpetuation of the existing Arab states are continually strengthening *wataniyya* at the expense of *qawmiyya*. Arab nationalism wished to reverse this order of things and strengthen *qawmiyya* at the cost of *wataniyya*. That is a basic problem facing the advocates of Arab unity: how to submerge *wataniyya* within *qawmiyya*.

There are ideologists and writers who stress that in terms of priorities the path to *qawmiyya* passes through *wataniyya*. Nasser was alive to the difficulty inherent in such an approach since patriotism of each Arab state may in the meantime be allowed to grow so strong as to resist submerging in *qawmiyya* or in an Arab unity. Therefore he demanded that Arab unity be achieved quickly, before the crystallisation of the individual Arab states. However, the view of giving precedence to *wataniyya* has become current recently. The individual Arab, it is argued, will learn of his attachment to pan-Arabism through his bond with his state. The tie with a particular state is intimate and concrete and only on its foundation will the link with pan-Arab nationalism be built. Figuratively, the erection of the wall of Arab unity as the political incarnation of *qawmiyya* needs first the solidification of the bricks of *wataniyya*.

In this emphasis on *wataniyya* extremes meet, as is advocated among some of the leftists, especially the communists, and in right-wing circles. The stress on *wataniyya* is today one of the hallmarks of the time, in which the ardour of the ideal of Arab unity has declined.

The complexity of the relationship between *qawmiyya* and *wataniyya* is basic in the Covenant. The Covenant emphasises Palestinian *wataniyya* together with the explanation that *qawmiyya* will not be weakened by it (Articles 12 and 13). On the other hand, Article 4 stresses eternity for Palestinism, i.e., *wataniyya*.

The Palestinians benefit from both worlds: Arab and Palestinian. Fundamentally, they are Arabs, culturally, ethnically and historically; however they claim that only in Palestine can they find a solution to their problem, and in consequence, the Arab states are, as it were, foreign countries for them. There are grounds for a rejoinder stressing that their link with the Arab nation leads to a conclusion that this country is not their only homeland, since they are partners in the overall Arab homeland. They or some of them could therefore also find the solution to their problem there, as actually many Palestinians have done. However, the Palestinians and the Arabs would not admit this. That is the difference between them and the Israelis, who have no other homeland. This also explains the Arab attempt to describe the countries of origin of the Israelis as their real homeland while arguing that the Palestinians have no other homeland than Palestine.

Article 2
Palestine, with the boundaries it had during the British Mandate, is an indivisible territorial unit.

This article is a continuation of the previous one and is designed to define 'Palestine' territorially. The very determination that 'Palestine' is an indivisible unit implies a demand for a unified state and a rejection of partition into Arab and Jewish states. Thus, the demand to liquidate Israel is implied in this statement. Many of the PNC's resolutions stress explicitly that the aim is 'the liberation of *all* the territory of Palestine.'

The expression 'with the boundaries it had during the Mandate' may be ambiguous since it is not clear whether Jordan is included in these borders. Initially, Jordan was part of the Palestine mandate but it was detached in 1922, being designated the Palestinian Trans-Jordan region, to which the Balfour Declaration would not apply. However, until May 1946 the reports of the Mandatory government to the League of Nations about Jordan continued to be included in the reports on Palestine.

When the Palestinian Covenant was drafted in 1964, the PLO contended that Jordan was not part of Palestine. The emblem of the PLO and the maps it published restricted Palestine to west of the River Jordan. This is also the stand expressed in the manifesto of 'the Political Bureau of the Revolutionary Forces for Joint Action'; this group became the left-wing of the Palestinian movement. This public statement, which was published in Beirut on 25 May 1964, declared: 'Palestine is that Arab land known in the political boundaries which existed under the oppressive British mandate prior to May 15, 1948' (American University of Beirut, *Arab Documents for 1964*, p. 253). In other words, the expression 'the period of the British mandate' means the end of the mandate.

Indeed, it could have been argued that the boundaries laid down in the mandate corresponded with the historical boundaries of Palestine as an ethnic unit and country. Since this was not the case, then Palestine as a political unit and the Palestinians as a people are the creation of a colonial settlement, which hereby is sanctified. The borders were not delineated according to the location of a Palestinian people, but they created the 'Palestinian people.' The parenthood of the Palestinian people was thus in a colonial settlement.

This article contains a time-bomb for the Palestinians and their political future, bound up with the problem of their link to Jordan. This problem has been on the PLO's agenda since its inception. The Palestinians on the East Bank constitute a large group of nearly 600,000 people, about 42 per cent of its population, of whom a part, and perhaps the majority, have been integrated in Jordan, assumed Jordanian citizenship and regard Jordan in a large measure as their home. The problem of the identity of the Palestinians in Jordan constitutes a difficulty that rules out a compromise between the PLO and Jordan. The PLO cannot allow itself to lose them, because they are the second largest Palestinian segment after the Palestinians of the West Bank. The Palestinians in Judea and Samaria are precluded from acquiescing in a situation under which their brethren in Jordan would be isolated in a different state, while Jordan for its part cannot allow the Palestinians in its country to owe allegiance to a political entity, probably hostile, outside its territory. This is a basic complication in which the whole Palestinian issue is enmeshed.

There are two possible ways of solving the problem: either by Jordan absorbing Palestine (the West Bank) thus transforming the Palestinians into Jordanians (as the Jordanian establishment hoped in claiming that Jordan was the successor of Palestine), or the absorption of Jordan by Palestine and its transformation into a part of Palestine. These two contradictory trends symbolise the basic contradiction between Hashemite Jordan and the PLO, but both are identical in regarding Jordan and Arab Palestine as one unit.

If the geographical partition between Jordan and Palestine was vague, the division in Jordan between 'Jordanians' as the original inhabitants of Jordan and 'Palestinians' as residents who have immigrated there, has been rather prominent, as far as the feeling and self-identification of the majority is concerned and as regards the distinction in law. The citizenship of the Palestinians who came to Jordan after 1948 is indeed specified in a different section of the Jordanian Nationality Law and so noted in their documents. Jordan granted citizenship to Palestinians living in its territory on 16 February 1954, provided they had Palestinian citizenship prior to May 1948—'Jews excepted,' as it is explicitly stated in the law. At a later date, on 2 February 1960, the right of obtaining citizenship was extended to every Palestinian who so desired.

Over the years, the Palestinians in Jordan have undergone a process of 'Jordanisation'. This process has also occurred in the residents of the West Bank, who acquiesced in being part of the Jordanian Kingdom and slowly began regarding Jordan as their country, even though many of them had reservations about its Hashemite regime. The PLO sought to stop this process of Jordanisation, by highlighting the special identity of the Palestinians. This process of assimilation was indeed interrupted on the West Bank, not through the influence of the PLO, but due to the 1967 war. It spilled over to the West Bank and strengthened Palestinian identity of the Palestinians there as well.

Even before the PLO was established, Shuqairy tried to gloss over the contradiction between his organisation and Jordan and cajoled its rulers into agreeing to the PLO's establishment by pleading that his organisation did not conspire to undermine the Jordanian entity. He used a formula of division of labour: namely that the PLO was an organization operating on the popular level, while Jordan was a governmental body and the homeland of the organisation (see his 'Ten Points' in *Documents on Palestine 1965*, pp. 414–15; *Palestine Yearbook* 1965, p. 61). The contradiction between Jordan and Palestine was obvious to both parties, even if they sought a *modus vivendi* of sorts, biding their time to break it up to each one's advantage. In fact, a dispute between the PLO and Jordan broke out and developed into an open row well before the Six Day War, and it continued thereafter.

The radical elements among the Palestinians, such as the Popular Front (the PFLP led by Dr Habash) were against the PLO placing too much stress on Palestinism in its doctrine. In their view, this contradicted the idea of Arab unity. The popular Front demanded that the PLO become an overall Palestinian–Jordanian organisation and that Jordanians be allowed to join Fedayeen organisations and the Palestinians professional associations. In the Agreement signed on 6 May 1970 by all Fedayeen organisations and the Palestinian professional the Jordanian regime, it was stated, probably to meet the PFLP's stand: '(The) Palestinian struggle is based on the belief that the people in the Palestinian–Jordanian theatre are one people . . .' (*International Documents on Palestine 1970*, p. 795).

At the 8th PNC, which met in February–March 1971, after the 'Black September' of 1970, in which the Fedayeen organisations were defeated and liquidated in Jordan, this development reached its apogee in a statement that Jordan and Palestine constituted a single unit, territorially and ethnically. It was even pointed out that the stress on Palestinism by the PLO was merely the tactic of a passing phase, while in fact Jordan and Palestine were one unit, both ethnically and geographically.

The resolution stated:

Jordan is linked to Palestine by a national relationship and a national unity forged by history and culture from the earliest times. The creation of one political entity in Transjordan and another in Palestine would have no basis either in legality or as to the elements universally accepted as fundamental to a political entity. It would be a continuation of the operation of fragmentation by which colonialism shattered the unity of our Arab nation and the unity of our Arab homeland after the First World War.

But this fragmentation has not prevented the masses, either west or east of the River Jordan, from feeling that they are one people, or from remaining united against the conspiracy of imperialism and zionism.

In raising the slogan of the liberation of Palestine and presenting the problem of the Palestine revolution, it was not the intention of the Palestine revolution to separate the east of the River from the west, nor did it believe that the struggle of the Palestinian people can be separated from the struggle of the masses in Jordan. It acted in conformity with the exigencies of a specific historical stage, with the object of concentrating on the direction of all forces towards Palestine so as to give prominence to our cause on Palestinian, Arab and international levels.

(*International Documents on Palestine 1971*, p. 398)

This resolution combines two statements: that the partition between Jordan and Palestine was artificial and that the very establishment of Palestine was a colonial act. There is thus an admission of the artificiality of the Palestinian entity and its colonial origin. In addition, it is pointed out that the Palestine–Jordan unity is included in the wider framework of Arab unity.

One major conclusion may be drawn from the above that the Palestinians will not admit: if Jordan and Palestine are one land and the Jordanians and Palestinians one people, then the Palestinians are not a people bereaved of a homeland, their struggle against Israel is not to liberate a homeland they do not possess, but to expand a homeland that they *do have*. Moreover, the very participation of Palestinians in the political life of Jordan is an expression of their self-determination, and thus their argument that they have no possibility of self-determination unless they regain the whole area of Palestine is spurious.

The ideologists of the PLO are sensitive to the argument that Jordan be regarded as their homeland. Its rejection is expressed in denigratory terms such as calling Jordan 'the alternative homeland' (*al-watan al-badīl*), i.e., an unreal or foster homeland.

The Palestine–Jordan unity is not emphasised in the resolutions of the subsequent Palestinian councils, but instead the need to maintain a 'Jordanian–Palestinian front' is reiterated, which in the last resort is designed to lead to some unity. The call of the 12th PNC (June 1974) may be taken as an example: '[The PLO will] struggle along with the Jordanian national forces to establish a Jordanian–Palestinian national front, whose aim will be to set up in Jordan a democratic national authority in close contact with the Palestinian entity that is established through the struggle' (*Journal of Palestine Studies*, Vol. 3, No. 4, Summer 1974, p. 224).

The stand of the PLO toward Jordan worsened. The PLO began calling blatantly for the overthrow of the Jordanian regime, thus adopting the stand of the more extreme organisations, such as the Popular Front and the Democratic Front. The Federation plan announced by King Hussein on 15 March 1972, under which the Jordanian Kingdom would be composed of a federation of two autonomous regions—the East Bank and the West Bank—was bluntly rejected as a direct threat to the PLO. Calls to overthrow the regime in Jordan and set up a national, democratic regime recurred in the resolutions of the Popular Congress and the 10th PNC (April 1972), the 11th PNC (January 1973), and the 12th PNC (June 1974). The rift between Jordan and the PLO thus became a political fact, which could no longer be papered over.

At the Rabat summit conference (26–29 October 1974), the PLO scored a political victory. It was unanimously recognised as the sole legitimate representative of the Palestinians. (In the Algiers summit conference a year earlier, the same resolution was adopted against Jordanian reservation.) Jordan's right to the West Bank as she had previously claimed under Security Council Resolution 242 to a certain exten' 'apsed in inter-Arab politics.

Nevertheless, these developments in the contest between Jordan and the PLO should not be regarded as final. The geopolitical circumstances in fact favour Jordan. The reason is that in order for a Palestinian state to be viable it must court Jordan's favours and may not be able to remain cut off from the kingdom. It is not accidental that at the end of 1976 Egypt advocated that there should be a 'link' between the Palestinian state and Jordan.

However, such a 'link' is not a connection between two equal bodies since the East Bank is more populous and developed and in consequence a Palestinian state on the West Bank may become subordinate to Jordan. The PLO leadership has forebodings on this score, as they understand that circumstances lean in favour of a 'Jordanian solution.' However, in the long run since the Palestinians will have a majority in such a union they may eventually stamp their character on it.

Article 3
The Palestinian Arab people possess the legal right to their homeland and have the right to determine their destiny after achieving the liberation of their country in accordance with their wishes and entirely of their own accord and will.

This is an abbreviated and combined version of Articles 3 and 4 in the 1964 charter. The right of the Palestinian people to their homeland is exclusive; hence it rules out that any other people may have a right or partnership in the same homeland. It too implies the demand for the demise of Israel. The decision over the type of internal regime or type of government is postponed until the post-liberation period. In the 1964 Covenant, this formula was designed to conciliate Jordan, i.e., that the issue whether it would be part of Jordan or independent was left open. However, it coincided with the Fatah demand of not engaging in ideological debates about the character of the regime of the liberated state at the present stage as it might split the Palestinians and divert their attention from the struggle against Israel (see Article 8 below). The expression 'to their homeland' means of course in its entirety. The phrase 'determine their destiny' (*yuqarrir masīrahū*) is the usual Arab expression for self-determination, thus in the translation of the Institute for Palestine Studies this sentence is rendered: 'shall exercise the right of self-determination.'

Self-determination of the Palestinians involves the entire homeland as spelled out in the preamble of the PLO's Ten-Point Programme which was adopted by the 12th PNC (June 1974):

"On the basis of the Palestinian National Charter and the Political Program drawn up at the Eleventh Session, held from January 6–12, 1973; and from its belief that it is impossible for a permanent and just peace to be established in the area unless our Palestinian people recover all their national rights and, first and foremost, their rights to return and to self-determination on the whole of the soil of their homeland" (see Appendix E).

The view that 'self-determination' will come *after* 'liberation' has been consistently held by the Jordanians to this day. Its practical meaning in Jordanian opinion has been that after Israel's withdrawal from the West Bank there would be a referendum to determine the nature of the regime; Jordanian rulers hope that the inhabitants of the West Bank will opt to link their fate with that of Jordan.

Article 4

The Palestinian identity is a genuine, essential and inherent characteristic: it is transmitted from parents to children, the Zionist occupation and the dispersal of the Palestinian Arab people, through the disasters which befell them, do not make them lose their Palestinian identity and their membership of the Palestinian community, nor do they negate them.

This statement is meant to thwart, ideologically, the possibility of assimilation of the Palestinians and the dissolution of their national entity, as a result of their dispersion or adoption of foreign citizenship, which would invalidate their claim to Palestine. This article thus complements the previous one. In original Arabic the three adjectives qualifying the Palestinian identity are *sifa asila lāzima lā tazūl*. They are rendered in the translation of the Institute for Palestine Studies as 'authentic, intrinsic and indissoluble.' Palestinian ownership of Palestine and their claim to the country are eternal. Palestinism, in this definition, is an everlasting affair, impervious to the vicissitudes of time. Palestinism has been transformed from a human, flesh and blood matter into a kind of metaphysical entity. This may also imply that the Palestinian existence is not a new affair and its future perpetuity purports to indicate the depths of its historicity. Thus, such a statement may have been designed to compensate for the fact that Palestinian nationalism is a new phenomenon and perhaps to counterbalance the continuous existence and the ancient origin of the Jews.

Shuqairy explained that any Palestinian who acquired foreign citizenship shall remain a Palestinian citizen with all his rights and obligations to his homeland (i.e., Palestine), no matter where he lives or works.

Thus, the Palestinians remain Palestinians, even if they acquire another citizenship and their link with Palestine overshadows their tie with the country of which they are citizens. Palestinism is independent of citizenship or nationality. On the contrary, Palestinian citizenship will follow from the characteristic of being Palestinian. This article provides the Palestinians with the right of 'dual loyalty,' which Article 23 of the Covenant indirectly condemns as regards the Jews. Furthermore, this and the following article constitute a Palestinian Arab counterpart to the Israeli Law of Return. This does not prevent Arab ideologists from finding the Israeli Law of Return inadmissible.

In the 1964 Covenant (Article 5) only the first half of the article was included. The supplement is designed to stress that the dispersal and the disasters that have befallen the Palestinians have not weakened their tie with Palestine. This assertion is meant to be descriptive or analytical though presumably it is normative, i.e., expressing an urge to inspire pride in their perseverence (*sumūd*).

Indeed, most Palestinians identify themselves as Palestinians even if they have set up homes in the Arab countries. Their maintenance of this identity is described here as derived from their very essence, but it can be assumed that a major factor that contributed to it has been the hostility they have met from Arab societies and the fact that the Palestinians have been regarded as second-class citizens in the Arab countries. Many complaints about this situation are found in Palestinian literature. A pamphlet of Fatah, an organisation that cannot be suspected of enmity to Arab nationalism, states: 'The persecution of the Palestinians in the Arab countries has been a factor that contributed to preserve the character of the Palestinian personality and reject assimilation' (*The Relationship between the Palestinian Revolution and the Arab and World Revolutions*, in the series 'Revolutionary Studies and Experiments,' p. 3).

It should be noted that the definition of the eternity of

Palestinism contradicts the prevailing conception in Arab nationalism that the Arab personality is the fundamental and permanent trait. Thus, Article 12 describes the preservation of the Palestinian identity as an exigency of the present stage of the struggle. In a resolution referring to the Jordan–Palestine question, the 8th PNC admitted that the partition (of Palestine) into these two countries was a fact of colonialism.

There are grounds for wondering how a colonialist carving out of the territory of Palestine is justified and made eternal on ethnic grounds.

Article 5
The Palestinians are those Arab nationals who, until 1974, normally resided in Palestine regardless of whether they were evicted from it or have stayed there. Anyone born after that date of a Palestinian father—whether inside Palestine or outside it— is also a Palestinian.

This is an article that is intended to supplement the theoretical stipulation concerning 'who is a Palestinian' and translate it into a legally binding meaning. For this purpose, a determining date is required. This date is not the end of the British Mandate in May 1948, but the year 1947, seemingly because immediately after the UN partition resolution in November 1947, as security was undermined through Arab attacks against the resolution, Arab families particularly of the middle and upper classes began deserting their homes for safe havens in the neighbouring countries. Latif Ghantus calls this emigration 'individual' (*fardiyeh*), i.e., an act of private initiative ('The influence of class composition on the Palestinian problem', *Dirāsāt 'Arabiyya*, Vol. 2, No. 2, December 1965, p. 43). Even the departure of those who left of their own choice is described here as eviction in accordance with the prevailing line in Palestinian historiography.

The juridical approach also involves an interpretation as to how Palestinism is passed on to the next generation. It was laid down, as customary in Islam, that Palestinism is handed down from father to son. Basically, the Palestinians are 'Arab citizens,' but the next article includes an exception.

Article 6
The Jews who had normally resided in Palestine until the beginning of the Zionist invasion will be considered Palestinians.

This article is a continuation of the previous one. It lays down that although, fundamentally speaking, the Palestinians are *Arabs*, there is a category of Jews, who had been living in the country before the Zionist invasion, who will also be considered as Palestinians. This implies that the Jews who are not regarded as Palestinians are aliens, who have no legally assured right to residence in the country and may therefore be asked to leave. The Covenant does not actually specify in which year the Zionist invasion began, but in the text of the resolutions of the 4th PNC in a chapter entitled: 'The Palestinian Struggle in the International Arena' (p. 51 in the official report of the council in Arabic), it is stated:

> 'The Assembly [i.e. the PNC Y.H.] affirms, moreover, that the aggression against the Arab nation and the territories of that nation, began with the Zionist invasion of Palestine in 1917, and that, as a consequence "the elimination of the consequences of the aggression" must signify the elimination of all such consequences since the beginning of the Zionist invasion and not merely since the June 1967 war. The slogan "the elimination of the consequences of the aggression" is therefore rejected in its present form, and must be replaced by the slogan "the destruction of the instrument of aggression". Thus, and thus alone, will "peace based on justice" be established.'
> (*International Documents on Palestine, 1968*, p. 403).

This definition of 'the beginning of the Zionist invasion' is repeated for example, by Yahia Hamūda, the acting chairman of the PLO Executive Committee after Shuqairy had resigned and before Yasser Arafat's appointment. He declared: 'The aggression against our land began in 1917 with the Balfour Declaration' (V. Vance et P. Laner, *Hussein de Jordanie: ma guerre avec Israël*, p. 166). The stipulation that the determining date for Jews is 1917 as against 1947 for the Arabs implies discrimination. The tolerable Jewish minority is the one that existed when the Balfour Declaration was issued and probably their offspring. The wheels of history must be turned back to nullify the consequences of the Zionist enterprise. This outlook is common in Palestinian political literature and is also reiterated in Article 20 below, which stipulates that the Balfour Declaration, the text of the Mandate and 'everything that has been based upon them, are deemed null and void.'

The question raised by this article is fundamental to the Arab cause, since the extent of the Arab character of 'liberated Palestine' is predicated on the reduction of the number of Jews. Back in the Mandate period, the traditional Arab stand was to demand independence for the country as a united Arab state with an assured, permanent Arab majority. To that end, the Arabs insisted, in addition to the termination of Jewish immigration, on a limitation of the number of Jews. For example, at the 1946 London Conference, the Arab delegate submitted a proposal on 19 September 1946 that the citizenship of independent Palestine be conferred on those Jews and Arabs: (1) who had Palestinian (Mandate) nationality before May 1936; and (2) who acquired such nationality after this date, on condition they had lived in the country ten years (i.e., they had arrived prior to 1946).

Palestinian political literature contains two main versions regarding the question of the fixing of the date for the quota of Jews who may be allowed to stay in the country: those who were living there before 1917 or before 1948. A hard-line version on this question exists in the Constitution of the Ba'th Party, the historic document of this movement promulgated in 1947. Article 11 stated: 'Whoever advocated or joined a racialist formation against the Arabs and whoever immigrated to the Arab homeland with a colonialist aim shall be expelled.' This applies to all Jews who immigrated to Palestine under the urge of Zionism which, according to the line prevailing in Arab nationalism, is identified with colonialism.

The basic stand of the late Mufti, Hāj Amīn al-Husseinī, was also that only the Jews who lived in the country before 1917 should stay. He said in an interview: 'The only solution . . . is the establishment of a national state composed of those residents of Palestine, Moslems, Christians and Jews, who were living there before the British conquest in 1917 and their offspring' ('Two interviews with Hāj Amīn' (al-Husseinī) in *Shu'un Filastiniyya*, No. 36, August 1974, p. 14). This approach is not new. As far back as 28 August 1947, a congress of Arab workers living in Haifa decided that the Jews who had been living in the country prior to 1917 and their offspring would be recognised as legal citizens.

In a book on the history of the Palestinian movement, Nāji 'Alūsh, Chairman of the Union of Palestinian Authors, pointed out: 'The stand of the Arab national movement on Palestine concerning the Jews can be summed up as follows: (1) The Jewish citizens (*al-muwātinūn*) have the right to participate in the independent government according to their numerical proportion in the population. They have been termed "original inhabitants of the homeland," their number did not exceed 20,000 and they did not own over one per cent of the land. They had lived in Palestine before the First World War. That is to say, immigrants who arrived after that war have no right to share in government' (*The Palestinian National Movement Vis-à-vis the Jews and Zionism, 1882–1948*, p. 170).

The appellation in this article of the Covenant of the Israelis, who today are 'Israeli Jews,' merely as Jews and not as Israelis is typical and consistent, because admission of 'Israeliness' means that a 'people' is in the process of formation as a national group (see commentary on Article 20).

This article amends the previous version of the 1964 Covenant that stated: 'Jews of Palestinian origin are considered Palestinians if they are willing to live peacefully and loyally in Palestine.'

The expression of 'origin' (in Arabic—*asl*) in the 1964 Covenant is apparently meant to exclude Jews who immigrated recently and were not 'original' Palestinian Jews. This expression is vague, but in view of its apposition to the previous article, which laid down the determining date for the Palestinism of the Arab as 1947, one could have inferred by analogy that the Jews of 'Palestinian origin' are those who lived in the country before 1948 and who could legally obtain Palestinian citizenship, i.e., those who had been living in the country before the British Mandate expired in 1948. It seems that such a definition accorded with Shuqairy's legal approach (a lawyer by profession) and in his autobiography he qualified the 'Palestinian Jews' as the 'legal citizens' (*Forty Years in Arab and International Life*, p. 500). This interpretation does not rule out the possibility that the intention in the 1964 Covenant was more extreme.

A corroborating view that 1948 is the cut-off date in the 1964

Covenant is found, for example, in a book written shortly before the PLO's establishment and the drafting of the original Covenant. The author was Niqula al-Dur, Shuqairy's deputy as chairman of the First Palestinian Congress, later a member of the PLO's Executive Committee and a member of the PLO's delegation to the Second Arab Summit Conference. His closeness to Shuqairy may have made him privy to his views. In his book, *Thus Lost and Thus to be Returned, the Role of the Oil and the Gun in the Liberation of Palestine*, (1963), al-Dur wrote, in the framework of 'a plan for a solution of the Palestinian problem': 'Permission to stay (in Palestine) should be granted to the Jews who shall declare that they are giving up the idea of the Jewish state and choose to stay in Palestine. Their number will be decided in the future, provided that it does not exceed the level of May 1948 and that priority be given to Jews from Arab lands. We do not have any obligation to keep a single Jew who entered Palestine after the end of World War I . . . We are doing this only as an act of humane participation in the solution of the problem and as a mark of our goodwill and desire to stabilize peace' (p. 272).

The expression 'if they desire to undertake to live in loyalty and peace,' which is included in the 1964 version, evokes the phrase in the well-known Article 11 of the UN General Assembly resolution of 11 December 1948, which states that 'the refugees wishing to return to their homes and live at peace with their neighbours should be permitted to do so.' Here, however, the expression is meant as a limiting criterion—only Jews who undertake to be loyal to the Palestinian state shall be recognised as Palestinians. An interpretation of this expression may be seen in the recurring motif in Palestinian literature which insists that the Jews who would be allowed in the democratic Palestinian state should relinquish Zionism and the idea of Jewish state-hood, as proof of their desire to live in peace. The limitation 'those who wish to live in peace' recurs as a condition for those Jews who shall remain in the democratic Palestinian state in accordance with the resolution of the 8th PNC (see below).

Even if the previous text of the 1964 Covenant is interpreted stringently as referring to Jews who had been living in Palestine before the Balfour Declaration, the revised version in the 1968 Covenant is even more strict. The very fact that the 4th PNC deemed it necessary to change the previous text and explicitly specify this restriction is significant. It cannot be assumed that this amendment was made cavalierly, since the alteration of an important document such as a covenant is the result of careful deliberation.

The Arab stand, as put forward by Arab and Palestinian spokesmen, did not merely demand that the Palestinians would return to Palestine; it also specified a condition that it would then be an Arab land *purified* of the alien population. Otherwise it would not be Arab and the Palestinians could not be its full masters.

Prof. Fayez Sayegh, a former member of the PLO Executive Committee, the founder of the PLO Research Centre in Beirut and presently an adviser to the Kuwaiti Government, formulated the target in these words: 'Peace in the land of Palestine and the neighbouring countries is our hearts' desire. Above all, a precondition for this is the liberation of Palestine, i.e., carrying out the condition of our return to Arab Palestine and the return of Palestine to us as an Arab land' (*A Handful of Mist, A Study of the Meanings of Bourghibism and its Slogans*, p. 19).

Shafīq al-Ḥūt, the head of the PLO office in Beirut, has expressed himself similarly: 'Ignoring the Arab entity is nothing but a part of the Imperialist-Zionist plan that aspires to liquidate the problem of the people of Palestine and deprive it of its right to struggle for the liberation of its usurped land, to restore it as a free Arab country to which its people return free, sovereign, powerful and respected' (*Facts about the Road to Liberation*, p. 6).

The expression 'restoring the land as an Arab country' is a turn of phrase frequent in Arab publications about the conflict.

Fatah proclamations have generally ended with the slogan: 'Long Live Free Arab Palestine'—a slogan stressing the Arab character that the population of the country should have.

Fatah spokesmen have explained their goal: 'The operation of liberation is not merely removing an imperialistic base, but what is more important: the extermination of a society (*inqirad mujtamai*); not only is military defeat the aim in the Palestinian war of liberation, but the liquidation of the Zionist character of the occupied land, whether in manpower or in society (*bashariyatan kanat am ijtima 'iyyatan*)' (*Liberation of the Occupied*

Lands and Method of Struggle Against Direct Colonialism,
p. 16–17; or *Fatah Yearbook for 1968,* p. 39).

The question of how to reduce the number of Jews in a
Palestinian state as a condition for preserving its Palestinian–
Arab character is, of course, not only a juridical matter; it
constitutes a fundamental dilemma in the Arab position. It is
not accidental that in Arab declarations in the past one could
note a link between the liquidation of Israel as a state (politicide)
and the liquidation of her Jewish inhabitants (genocide), highlighted by the use of murderous terms against the Israelis
(putting an end, eradicating, throwing into the sea, etc.) This
article, in both versions, evades this difficulty by reducing the
number of Jews by means of an elegant juridical definition.

The reduction of the Jewish population is not necessarily to be
carried out only through violence. Shuqairy often made the
proposal to send the Jews back to their countries of origin. Nāji
'Alūsh repeats this proposal: 'Why not demand from the nations
of the world to seek an appropriate place where the Jews would
live, without this being at the expense of any other people?
Why not ask the United Nations to finance this plan?' (*The
Road to Palestine,* p. 219). ('Alush ignores the fact that his
remarks imply recognition of the Jews as a national and not just
a religious group.)

A Fatah manifesto of 19 October 1968 states: 'Our struggle
aspires to liberate the Jews themselves of the burden of intel-
lectual terror and racialist robbery, which the Zionist movement
implements against the Jews of the world. Therefore our revolution, which believes in the freedom and dignity of men,
considers first and foremost the laying of bases, which would
enable the radical uprooting of Zionism and the liquidation of
the conquest of the Zionist settlers in all forms. At the same time,
its aim is to outline a humane programme that will enable the
Jews to live a human dignified life, as they had always lived
under the auspices of the Arab state and Arab society' (*Fatah
Yearbook for 1968,* p. 157). The Jews of Palestine must therefore
be restored to being a minority, as they had been in the Arab
states. Such an approach takes us back to the traditional status
of the Jews as *dhimi,* a protected humiliated community in the
Islamic state.

The amendment of Article 6 in the 1968 Covenant has great

significance. This has been attested by *The Palestine Yearbook*, *1968* published by the Institute for Palestine Studies in Beirut, whose orthodoxy on the Palestinian issue is not to be questioned. The Yearbook endorses the interpretation that the intention in the amended article is to limit the number of Jews in the country to those who had lived there before 1917, even though the article in the Covenant does not specify a year, and that the intention in the 1964 Covenant was less stringent. It reads: 'One of the important amendments of the Palestinian National Covenant is Article 6 . . . which replaces Article 7 (in the 1964 Covenant) . . . From the resolutions of Fourth Palestinian National Council of 1968 one can conclude that the aggression against the Arab nation and its land began with the Zionist invasion of Palestine in 1917 and that eradication of the traces of aggression must mean the removal of all traces of this aggression that has continued since the onset of the Zionist invasion and not just since the June War [of 1967]. Hence, it should be understood that the Palestinian National Covenant considers as Palestinians only those Jews who lived in Palestine before 1917' *(The Palestine Yearbook, 1968,* Arabic, Beirut, 1971, p. 71).

The interpretation that the version of this article in the 1968 Covenant is stricter than the original Covenant is thus not an arbitrary Israeli explanation. For example, it is also the interpretation of Sabri Jiryīs, previously a member of the al-Ard organisation, who after he had left Israel became a researcher at the PLO Research Centre in Beirut and recently reappeared as the candidate for heading a PLO office in Washington. Jiryīs discusses the contradiction between the principle of the 'democratic state' (see below) and the fact that this article of the Covenant had not been amended since the 4th PNC: 'The first thing that has to be done is to abolish or amend the famous Article 6 in the revised Covenant of 1968. The only possible interpretation of this article is the uprooting of 99 per cent of the Jews who live in Palestine today; this causes great damage to the Palestinians in various progressive circles in the world. There is no need, nor logic in retaining this article in its present form, which indicates an exaggerated toughening of our stand (*tashaddud mubāligh*) in comparison with the earlier article in the original Covenant' (*Al-Nahar*, Beirut, 15 May 1975).

The question arises: what impelled the 4th PNC to amend this article in such a restrictive fashion that only Jews who had lived in Palestine before 1917 would be recognised as Palestinians? Why was the previous formula unsatisfactory to the point where it had to be revised and the limitation fixed so harshly? Surely, debates must have taken place in the 4th PNC as to why the article should be changed, as there are articles that were not altered from their original version. For a clear-cut reply we have to wait until the testimonies of participants at the Council are published, especially the members of the 'Covenant Committee,' which was appointed to propose the revision of the text. For the moment, one can only put forward hypotheses: Israel's victory in the Six Day War highlighted Israel's importance and the qualitative advantage of the Jewish population. The Jewish population must therefore be reduced in order that the country should be Arab after liberation. Perhaps the influence of the younger generation and the Fedayeen organisations at the 4th PNC and the aim of attracting the rising generation to the PLO created the need for a more clear-cut wording than that in the comparable article of the 1964 Covenant. Doctrinal consistency urged that if Zionism was depraved and if all the arrangements made after 1917 were rejected, including the resolutions of the League of Nations and the United Nations, then their practical outcome in the form of Jewish immigration must also be eradicated.

THE CONCEPT OF THE DEMOCRATIC STATE

The radical attitude embodied in Article 6 of the 1968 Covenant became an obstacle in the PLO's public relations. The article served as proof that the Arab stand had not been moderated nor become reasonable after the 1967 war, as claimed by many Arab spokesmen. The slogan of the democratic state in which Muslims, Christians and Jews will live peacefully together was devised as proof that the Palestinian state would not discriminate against the Jews, even though at first it was not always made clear exactly how many Israeli Jews would be permitted to become its citizens.

Back in the time of the British Mandate, Palestinian leaders proclaimed that the independent Palestinian state would be 'democratic.' Such democracy meant that its regime would be determined by its Arab majority. There was also the implication that the Jewish minority would be granted civil rights, according to its numerical proportion, which would, however, be frozen by ending immigration. 'Democracy' was extolled as proof of the progressiveness of Palestinian national aims. Fatah reaffirmed this aim in a memorandum to the UN dated 17 October 1968: 'The establishment of an independent and sovereign democratic state, in which all legal citizens would benefit from equal rights, irrespective of religion or language' (*Fatah Yearbook, 1968*, p. 148). It should be noted that the qualification of 'legal citizens' does not contradict the numerical restriction in both versions of the Covenant. As against the democratic Palestinian state, Israel has been denigrated as undemocratic, because it rests on discrimination in that its aim is a Jewish state.

The notion of a democratic state was brandished by Palestinian spokesmen with the implication that the Jewish population of Israel would be allowed to stay.

The Democratic Front of Naif Hawattma proposed to the 6th PNC (September 1969) to amend the Covenant and enshrine the idea of the democratic state in it. This proposal was rejected by the PNC. The 7th PNC (June 1970) charged the Executive Committee to study the issue and put its proposal before the next PNC. Finally the 8th PNC (28 February–5 March 1971) passed the following resolution:

> The Palestinian armed struggle is neither a racial nor a sectarian struggle against the Jews. That is why the future state in the Palestine liberated from Zionist colonialism will be the democratic Palestinian state, where those wishing to live peacefully in it would enjoy equal rights and obligations within the framework of the aspirations of the Arab nation to national liberation and complete unity, with emphasis on the unity of the people on both banks of the River Jordan.
>
> (*Fateh*, March 23, 1971, p. 14)

This resolution is put forward by Palestinian spokesmen as a radical change of position and as if it constitutes an amendment of Article 6, since this change appears to allow all the Israeli Jews to stay in the Palestinian state. Palestinian spokesmen also praise Arafat's remarks at the United Nations:

> In my capacity as Chairman of the Palestine Liberation Organization and commander of the Palestinian revolution I

proclaim before you that when we speak of our common hopes for the Palestine of tomorrow we include in our perspective all Jews now living in Palestine who choose to live with us there in peace and without discrimination.'

(*Journal of Palestine Studies*, Vol. 4 No. 2, Winter 1975, p. 191)

The conception of the democratic state is being used by the PLO spokesmen to display moderation, compromise and a generous humane approach, which shows consideration for the Israelis, despite their sharing in the crime of Zionism. It is thus seen by some as an attempt to introduce relativity into the PLO absolutist stand. However in reality this slogan is nothing but a euphemism for the old demand for the demise of Israel as a political body. Arab spokesmen boast that the democratic state is a fair compromise in which in return for the Arabs' magnanimous readiness to accept the Israeli Jews in their state, the Israelis have to concede their state and their existence as a nation. The democratic state would thus grant the Jews the status the Jews have in the Diaspora, who are Jews in consciousness but not in their political distinctiveness, or it seeks to exile the Israeli while he is still living in his national homeland. There is thus no real compromise. A true conciliatory stand would only consist of Arab readiness to coexist with Israel as a state and not with its remnants.

In the resolution of the 8th PNC, the restriction on the number of Israeli Jews that shall be permitted to live in the Palestinian state becomes as it were voluntary limitation, dependent on the desire of those Israelis 'who wish to live peacefully.' However, these Jews will have to acquiesce in the fact that the Palestinian state will be *Arab* and perhaps united with Jordan and the rest of the Arab world. By such a unity their proportion in the population of the country will diminish and its Arab character shall thus be reinforced. In their publications, the Palestinians point out that this state must not in any way be deviant because of the Jewish element in its population, since this may make the union with the Arab states difficult. Therefore, such a state should not be bi-national as some commentators explained mistakenly, and certainly not multi-national, but explicitly and emphatically an *Arab* state with a minority of Jews, who from a national viewpoint would become *Arabs*—Arabs of the Jewish faith.

In the Covenant, furthermore, the resolution of the 8th PNC did not refer to Article 6 at all as its amendment or replacement. The resolution exists *alongside* Article 6 which remains valid. The fact that the Covenant has not been amended to include the principle of the democratic state is significant, principally because the proposals to amend it were rejected.

The issue of the democratic state gave rise to a fierce debate within the PLO. Not all the Palestinian organisations agreed to the principle of the democratic state as the final Palestinian objective. Several of them, such as the 'Popular Front,' the 'Arab Liberation Front,' the 'Popular Front-General Command,' the 'Popular Armed Struggle' and Dr Sartawi's 'Executive Committee for the Liberation of Palestine' sharply criticised it. These organisations were ready to accept it as a tactical slogan and a public relations ploy. They were concerned that should it be adopted as a principle it would have entailed a large number of Israeli Jews remaining in the country, which would impair its Arabness, moreover, the country was too narrow to include the Palestinians and the Israelis and since the right of the Palestinians predominates there is no escape but that many Israelis would have to make room for the returning Palestinians. (For details of this debate, see the article: 'The meaning of "a democratic Palestinian state" ' in the author's *Palestinians and Israel*, 1974.)

In a lecture called 'The Palestine of Tomorrow' given at a symposium in Kuwait held on 13–17 February 1971, (which was published in Beirut in the *Fateh* periodical (in English) Volume 3, No. 1 (23 March 1971), Dr Nabil Sha 'ath, (Director of the PLO's Planning Centre) analysed the arguments of the Fedayeen organisations that opposed the idea of the democratic state (particularly the Arab Liberation Front and the Popular Front). Sha 'ath pointed out: 'The attack [on the idea of the democratic state, Y.H.] was so virulent, however, as to force other organisations into defensive positions. Such a state of paralysis delayed the Palestine National Congress from amending Article 6 of the Covenant, thus giving the Zionists a windfall opportunity to attack the democratic state on the basis of Palestinian inconsistency and tactical manoeuvring' (p. 9).

It is significant that Sabri Jiryis (in the article already cited above) categorically demands the amendment of Article 6 and in no way considers that the resolution of the 8th PNC can be considered as constituting such an amendment. Even though a Council's resolution is of a binding character, it does not attain the prominence of a principle that is enshrined in the Covenant. The very fact that an amendment in the Covenant requires a two-thirds majority vote of members of the Council, while ordinary resolutions are passed by a simple majority of those present, gives the Covenant greater weight, and in a case of conflict between a PNC resolution and the Covenant it can be argued that the Covenant will prevail. Significant here are the remarks of Sha 'ath that the opposition to the idea of a democratic state, which was to replace Article 6, did in fact prevent its amendment.

It should be noted that only the resolution of the 8th PNC on the democratic state had numerical significance with regard to the Israeli Jews who would be allowed to remain in it, in contradiction to the limitation in Article 6. In later PNC resolutions the democratic state is dealt with summarily without examining its significance. *Prima facie* there have been grounds for expecting that the principle of the democratic state as the final objective and the crowning achievement of PLO thinking would be allocated a prominent place in PNC resolutions and that its details be elaborated especially when other issues are so repetitively discussed at great length in PNC resolutions and whole paragraphs are devoted to them. This is not the case as regards the democratic state. The resolutions of the 9th PNC did not mention the subject at all. A change occurred in the political platform of the Popular Congress and the 10th Council where reference was made to the establishment of a 'democratic society.' The change surely did not occur unpremeditatedly, but was apparently intended to placate the opponents of the very idea of establishing a separate Palestinian state that contradicted the trend towards Arab unity by increasing the number of Arab states instead of decreasing them. The same phrase recurs in the 'PLO's Political Programme' which was approved at the 11th PNC (January 1973) as a final crystallisation of its outlook: 'To continue the struggle . . . for the establishment of a Palestinian democratic society which guarantees the right to work and a decent life for all citizens so they can live in equality, justice and fraternity, in a democratic society opposed to all forms of prejudice due to race, colour or creed' (*Palestine Lives*, p. 162). The 12th PNC acquitted itself by stating: 'Any step taken toward liberation is a step toward the realisation of the Liberation Organisation strategy of establishing the democratic Palestinian state specified in the resolutions of the previous Palestinian National Councils' (see Appendix E, and Article 4).

After the 'Liberation', all Palestinians will be invited to return, even those whose permanent residence is in other countries, and demand property that they had owned before 1948. Their return is described in warm terms as return to their 'homes'. The conflict inevitably occurring between the Jews now living on that land and the incoming Palestinians would be decided in favour of the Palestinians by the liberated Palestinian government. Such an intention can be deduced from the platform submitted by the Political Committee of the Popular Congress that preceded the 10th PNC in April 1972. It stated: 'In [the democratic society, i.e., state Y.H.] the interests will be safeguarded of all social groups which participated in the revolution, supported it or even only contented themselves with sympathising with it, without collaborating with the enemy or facilitating his task in occupying our territory and suppressing our compatriots' (Official Report in Arabic, PLO, *The Palestinian Popular Congress and Tenth Extraordinary Council, 6–12 April, 1972*, p. 84). The Israelis certainly do not support the 'Palestinian revolution,' and thus their interests would not be safeguarded.

In this way, evidently, the PLO solves for itself the problem of the large numbers of Jews in liberated Palestine. Cities such as Lydda, Beersheba, Ramleh, Jaffa and Acre and parts of Haifa will be restored to their previous Arab proprietors and their Jewish population would be evicted. Indeed, from the Arab viewpoint, it is preferable to insist on the principle of restoring land property to the Arabs, instead of getting embroiled in decrees restricting the number of Jews who are allowed to remain.

The phrase in the 'Political Programme of the PLO' concerning the assurance of rights in the democratic society to 'all citizens who live in equality, justice and fraternity' may also refer to such a policy. The demand of the Israeli Jews to keep land is not 'equality and justice.' Remarks to this effect may have been alluded to in the speech of Arafat at the UN which expressed consent to live 'with all Jews now living in Palestine who choose to live with us there in peace and without discrimination.' The claim of the Israeli Jews to keep their homes, in which they lived since 1948, is discriminatory against the returning Arab refugees.

Thus the establishment of the 'democratic' Palestinian state is bound up with a mass evacuation of Jews from their homes, and they will be thus forced to emigrate. *The 'democracy' that is allegedly intended to assure the rights of the Israeli Jews to live in the Palestinian state is also the instrument of dispossessing them.* 'The return' as a chief PLO slogan embodies at one and the same time the Arab objective and the means of achieving it. The very 'return' will change 'Israel' into 'Palestine' and the right of return for the Palestinians boils down to a euphemistic expression of a right to *subvert* the state of Israel.

In presenting triumphantly the idea of the democratic state at the UN, Arafat did not succeed in hiding its true meaning. It became obvious that the use of the term 'democratic state' was nothing but a euphemism for the demise of Israel and that such a state was meant to replace Israel. When Arab propagandists were pressed on this point, they argued that the democratic state was merely 'a dream and a vision,' quoting in support Arafat's remark: 'Why, therefore, should I not dream and hope? For is not revolution the making of dreams and hopes?' (*Journal of Palestine Studies*, Vol. 4, No. 2, Winter, 1975, p. 191).

However, the democratic state is not a vague, innocent, utopian vision but a topic in whose implementation the Palestinians are preoccupied continuously; it is not a dream but a plan of action. Dr 'Omar Maḥjūb explains in an article in *Shu'un Filastiniyya* the PLO monthly (January–February 1975) called 'Democratic Palestine—the Aim, the Plan and Historical Necessity': 'Democratic Palestine, in addition to being a goal, is also a plan of battle and liberation.' Prior to this, he states: 'The Zionist entity must disappear. After this entity has been overthrown, settlers only will remain behind, who will be in the nature of the former Israelis. In order to become citizens in the new Palestine, they will have to be assimilated in it . . . hence, democracy is a goal and plan of action simultaneously.' The democratic state is therefore a plan for granting some Israelis the right to assimilate in the Palestinian-Arab state established on the ruins of Israel, and stop being Israelis, even though they may preserve their Jewish religion.

Article 7

That there is a Palestinian community and that it has material, spiritual and historical connections with Palestine are indisputable facts. It is a national (qawmī) duty to bring up Palestinians in an Arab revolutionary manner. All means of information and education must be adopted in order to acquaint the Palestinian with his country in the most profound manner, both spiritual and material that is possible. He must be prepared for the armed struggle and ready to sacrifice his wealth and his life in order to win back his homeland and bring about its liberation.

On the one hand, this article stresses the bond between the Palestinians with Palestine as permanent, in the same spirit as Article 4. On the other hand, Article 7 insists on the need to foster an awareness of this tie. The draft of the Palestinian National Organisation prepared by the Palestine Experts Commission of the Arab League in 4 July 1962, stated: 'The action for the liberation of Palestine necessitates preserving the Palestinian people and its components and maintaining its personality, as there is no homeland without a people.' Resolutions of the early PNCs gave prominence to nationalist indoctrination in a series of educational activities, while in later Councils the centre of gravity shifts to political and organisational activities. The educational activities are described here as a national pan-Arab duty (*qawmī*), which is superior to the national duty in the limited Palestinian sense (*watanī*).

This article was redrafted in the 1968 charter. The first sentence is an addition. Compared with the previous version, the bond to the homeland is presented as a fact, not merely as an aspiration. In the second sentence, the phrase 'national education' (*qawmī*) has been altered to 'revolutionary education.' This change and the additional phrase 'preparation for the armed struggle and sacrifice' are in the Fedayeen spirit, which found expression at the 4th PNC in which the Fedayeen organisations participated en bloc for the first time. Education does not mean fostering an abstract attachment to the cause, but is a concrete commitment expressed in acts of struggle and sacrifice. As the ideologists of Fatah contended, combat will generate patriotism and not the other way round. Shuqairy wanted the PLO to concentrate on preparatory activities to make the Palestinians qualified to participate in the 'War of Liberation,' while the Fedayeen organisations demanded the launching of independent battle operations at once, claiming that these activities would forge the Palestinians into a fighting people. National education does not precede combat, but is realised by and through it.

Article 8
The phase in their history, through which the Palestinian people are now living, is that of national (watanī) struggle for the liberation of Palestine. Thus the conflicts among the Palestinian national forces are secondary, and should be ended for the sake of the basic conflict that exists between the forces of Zionism and of Imperialism on the one hand and the Palestinian Arab people on the other. On this basis the Palestinian masses, regardless of whether they are residing in the national homeland or in Diaspora (mahājir) constitute—both their organisations and the individuals —one national front working for the retrieval of Palestine and its liberation through armed struggle.

Internal divisions on social and ideological issues must be put off for the sake of concentration on the struggle against Israel. The style of 'secondary contradiction' and 'basic contradictions' shows the influence of the language of Fatah and the younger generation. The previous version (Article 9) said: 'Doctrines, whether political social or economic, shall not occupy the people of Palestine from the primary duty of liberating their homeland.'

The main, basic contradiction with Israel, called 'antagonistic contradiction' in the language of the left, is an absolute one that excludes the possibility of a compromise. However, the other contradictions are relative and transitory because beside them there is also a region of common interest. The conception that there is an absolute contradiction between the Arabs and Palestinians on the one hand and Israel on the other rules out the possibility of a political settlement by compromise and calls for a war to the bitter end. 'The Political Programme of the PLO' enacted by the 11th PNC makes the following assertion: 'Such an antagonistic contradiction with the Zionist enemy cannot be resolved except through revolutionary violence' (*Palestine Lives*, p. 158).

The phrase 'the phase . . . of the national struggle' is meant to stress, in the spirit of Fatah thought, that the social struggle to determine the character of the internal social regime should be postponed until a future date, i.e., after liberation, as the 'liberation of the land' precedes the 'liberation of man.' This issue was a bone of contention between Fatah and the radical groups, such as the 'Popular Front.' The latter argued that a distinction between these two stages was 'mechanistic' as there was a 'dialectical link' between them and the masses would join up wholeheartedly only if they were convinced that the liberation of the land merged with their social liberation. Thus, the social goals are actually relevant to the political struggle for liberation and cannot be postponed to the future.

Another bone of contention throughout the period was whether the Palestinians can be considered as forming a single front in the struggle against Israel. Fatah's reply was in the affirmative. It thus followed the point of view of Shuqairy who had wanted to turn the PLO into a popular all-embracing organisation of the Palestinians irrespective of origin and social classes, since all were 'natural' members in the PLO by virtue of being Palestinians. The definition in Article 8 is also all-inclusive, with the distinction that the 1964 version referred to all Palestinians, i.e., as individuals constituting one front, whereas the 1968 version uses the term 'Palestinian masses' as constituting such a front, which may signify a more collective corporate approach.

The left-wing organisations (like the 'Popular Front' and subsequently the 'Democratic Front') differentiated between the proletarian class, which is wholeheartedly devoted to the struggle, and the Arab and Palestinian bourgeoisie, especially the wealthy bourgeoisie, whose community of interests with imperialism blunts its antagonism against Israel and by its very nature is not ready to make sacrifices for the struggle. Thus, it could not be relied on and should be left out. However, according to the leftish principles of the 'United Front,' it was argued that the *petite bourgeoisie* could be included in the revolutionary organisation, on condition that its participation was at the grass-roots level (*qā'ida*) and not in the leadership (*qiyāda*).

The problem of defining the sections of the Palestinian society participating in the struggle was raised in the Agreement of 6 May 1970. This Agreement, which served as a platform, was endorsed for the first time after the 4th PNC by all the Fedayeen organisations, including the 'Popular Front' of Dr Habash (PFLP), who had previously quitted the PLO and did not attend the 5th and 6th PNCs. The Popular Front acceding to this agreement marked the beginning of the Popular Front's return to the PLO. The agreement laid down: 'The forces of the Palestinian revolution are the toiling Palestinian masses and all forces which have an interest in the stage of national liberation of the soil of Palestine' (*International Documents on Palestine, 1970*, p. 795). Having an interest in liberation is rather a vague specification which can be interpreted widely.

Another division between the Palestinians is territorial: according to their places of residence. This division was not referred to in the 1964 version of the Covenant. There was no difficulty in stating that all Palestinians were partners in the struggle, including presumably those living under Israeli rule. The 1968 amended version includes a reference to the territorial distribution of the Palestinians between those in 'the occupied land'—an expression that could cover both the Arabs in the administered areas and the Israeli Arabs because even in its pre-1967 borders Israel was commonly termed 'the occupied land'. —and the other Palestinians, who are described as being in 'exile' or diaspora. It should be noted that in Palestinian literature the Israeli Arabs who have previously been treated with suspicion and disrespect are too described as belonging to the PLO Front. These Arabs are, according to the present mood, even praised because of their alleged suffering in the Jewish state and their persistence in carrying on the struggle.

The question of how to create the 'United Front' has been a constant bone of contention. In Shuqairy's time, there was considerable opposition to the PLO among the Palestinians. Since the 4th PNC, the PLO has become a framework for organisations that are essentially Fedayeen groups, who have been bitterly divided among themselves. The opposition has become internal, and the issue of unity has preoccupied many of the Palestinian National Councils.

The 'Popular Front,' one of the important Palestinian organisations, has alternately left and rejoined the PLO and on 26 September 1974 announced that it was leaving the PLO Executive Committee (not the PNC). Internal disputes in the PLO hampered the operation of the organisations and repeatedly caused the postponement of meetings of the Council, which was convened only if there was prior assurance that some consensus could be reached. The internal disputes also led to the resolutions being based on a compromise as a common denominator between the Fedayeen organisations, excluding controversial issues. The dispute between the mainstream of the PLO and the organisations constituting the 'Rejection Front', (and also the Lebanese war) prevented the convening of the 13th NPC for nearly three years, from June 1974 until March 1977. Indeed, all the Fedayeen organisations, including the Rejection Front, participated in the 13th Council. However, while the Arab Liberation Front (created by the Iraqi Ba'th party) returned to take part in the PLO's Executive Committee set up at this council, the Popular Front continued to boycott it.

Article 9
Armed struggle is the only way to liberate Palestine. Thus it is the overall strategy, not merely a tactical phase. The Palestinian Arab people assert their absolute determination and firm resolution to continue their armed struggle and to work for an armed popular revolution for the liberation of their country and their return to it. They also assert their right to normal life in Palestine and to exercise their right to self-determination and sovereignty over it.

This is a new article which was designed to define the operational principles for the achievement of the objective. The extremism of the goal of liquidation of the state of Israel and 'liberation' of its territory rules out the possibility of a political solution, which by its very nature is one of compromise. This is the logic of this article and Article 21. The only course is one of violence.

In Shuqairy's Covenant the principles of a programme of

action for the struggle against Israel were not elaborated. In those days, the matter seemed remote. According to Shuqairy's conception, the struggle against Israel was military, in the mode of conventional warfare and it would be an inter-Arab war in the framework of the Arab League. Thus launching the war was dependent on the state of preparedness of the Arab armies and subject to a decision by the Arab states. The Palestinian Liberation Army (PLA), which Shuqairy founded, was an adjunct to the armies of the Arab states and originally under the inter-Arab High Command. Shuqairy considered that the main aims of the PLO should be the organisation of the Palestinians in the political field, highlighting their problem on the Arab and international level, and the establishing, equipping and training of a Palestinian army. Thus PLO focused on organisation and preparations. The Fedayeen organisations sharply criticised Shuqairy's approach, which meant, practically speaking, the subordination of the struggle to the Arab League. They had a negative and derogatory view of the League as split by endless dissensions and consequently a worthless body. They argued that such subordination would only implant the disputes that had paralysed the League into the Palestinian organisations and that dependence on the League would be detrimental to the Palestinian cause. In their view too, the struggle against Israel must be military, but it should be in the form of *guerrilla* warfare. Consequently, such a struggle could start immediately, and the Palestinians could initiate it on their own. The roles were thus reversed: the Palestinians were not a junior force that would operate as a supplement to the Arab armies, but instead the Arab states and their armies would support the Palestinians. Stressing the role of the Palestinians in the fighting also reflected the weakness of the Arab armies after the Six Day War. The Palestinian people, according to this article, was therefore proclaiming that it would continue the struggle, even if the Arab states would not be playing an active part in it.

This article reiterates statements in the resolutions of a conference called by Fatah and a number of other Fedayeen organisations in Cairo in January 1968: 'The armed struggle is the only way to liberate Palestine. It rests on the Palestinian people—as its vanguard and foundation—and on the Arab people as a big support that provides reassurance through training, preparation, equipment and participation' (*Fatah Yearbook 1968*, p. 128).

Political action is not mentioned in this article in the Covenant. However, the very stress on the military path as the main strategy implies that the political means are ancillary. In Fatah language, the armed struggle is the infrastructure while the political action is the superstructure. This is the opposite of Clausewitz's aphorism that politics is the continuation of the armed struggle by other means. Thus, political means must tally with the military struggle, from which they are derived. The armed struggle here means guerrilla warfare.

The phrase 'strategy and not tactics' comes from the Fatah lexicon (see the author's *Fedayeen Action and Arab Strategy*, p. 8). The same expression is also found in the charter of the organisations that met in Cairo in January 1968 (Article 7). This expression signifies that guerrilla warfare by the Fedayeen is not an auxiliary activity, such as commando operations that sometimes were launched as an adjunct to regular warfare, but constitutes the main mode of operation, and that such warfare by itself can achieve the goal of defeating Israel.

It should be noted that in the text of the resolutions of the 4th PNC the relationship is less one-sided. Politics supplements the armed struggle, but also directs it: 'Palestinian armed struggle for the liberation of our usurped homeland is incomplete unless there is political action to complement it. This political action is the foundation of armed struggle; it defines its aims and explains to the masses why it adopts specific attitudes setting its individual action in their proper perspective. In affirming this fact, the Assembly [i.e., the 4th PNC, Y.H.] calls on all forces and elements taking part in the struggle to act in conformity with this political action and be guided by it' (*International Documents on Palestine, 1968*, p. 400). Thus the supremacy of politics served as a justification for the demand of the PLO's establishment at that time from all the Palestinian parties to accept its authority as the political leadership.

'The armed popular revolution' signifies the participation of the people in the struggle against Israel and is depicted as the culmination reached by the mere expansion of the operations of the Fedayeen, who in Fatah language are 'guides' and the 'vanguard,' whose role is to 'kindle' the revolution until it spreads and embraces all ranks of the people (see below in Article 10).

The expression 'normal life' is meant to affirm that the life of the Palestinians outside of their homeland is defective and abnormal causing their self-alienation (see also below Article 17).

The phrases 'sovereignty over the country' and 'right to self-determination' are complementary, as from achieving sovereignty the actualisation of self-determination will result. The expression *taqrīr al-masīr*, literally meaning a definition of what will happen in the future, or determination of fate, is ordinarily translated as self-determination. Total liberation and the ruling out of the possibility of coexistence with Israel, whatever her size or shape, stem from the right of self-determination for the Palestinians. Thus, self-determination for the Palestinians becomes a euphemism for the liquidation of Israel. It is probably in this sense that many Palestinians and Arabs understand UN General Assembly's resolutions' recognition of self-determination for the Palestinian people, and see their 'right of return' as a warrant, even if vague and equivocal, issued by the international community for Israel's demise or something close to it.

Changes in wording and emphasis have occurred in the definitions of the essence of the struggle against Israel. Paradoxically, the difficulties the Fedayeen organisations had in launching incursions from the Jordanian border perhaps contributed to the stressing of the importance of their special mode of combat. The agreement of 6 May 1970 stated: 'Popular revolutionary war is the principal course to the liberation of Palestine' (*International Documents on Palestine, 1970*, p. 795). This formula was apparently intended to gratify the Popular Front. The 7th PNC (June 1970) stated: 'The military solution is the only solution for the present conflict between us and the Zionist entity' (*Ibid.*, p. 824). At an extraordinary emergency session of the PNC (August 1970), it was reaffirmed that 'the liberation of Palestine and the other Arab occupied territories could only be achieved through armed struggle and a long-term people's war' (*Ibid.*, p. 896). This formulation was influenced by the aim of this session which was to protest against the acceptance by Egypt and Jordan of what was called the 'Rogers' plan.' Subsequently this Egyptian move influenced the formulation that was passed at the 8th Council (March 1971), which expressed a moderation of the outlook regarding the centrality of Fedayeen warfare: 'The armed struggle undertaken by the revolutionary vanguards of the Palestinian people at the outset of 1965 [meaning the guerrilla war escalating to a comprehensive popular war of liberation] is the principal form of the struggle for the liberation of Palestine. Joint action by regular troops and commando forces in the armed struggle is more liable to realise the victorious popular revolution. All other forms of struggle should be parallel to the armed struggle' (*Fateh*, 23 March 1971, p. 14). Hostilities are thus to begin with guerrilla fighting but to culminate in mixed guerrilla and conventional warfare. This definition indicates that the Arab states are partners and not merely auxiliaries. Conventional warfare was therefore elevated in status. On the other hand, it can be assumed that terror, in the view of PLO leaders, was included in the category of the 'revolutionary violence.'

In the wake of the 1973 war, which increased the prestige of the regular Arab armies and in which the Palestinians played a minor role (although in their writings they try to portray it as a larger one), the stress on the armed struggle was toned down further: 'The Liberation Organisation will employ all means and first and foremost armed struggle . . .' (Article 2 in the Ten-Point Programme approved by the 12th PNC on 9 June 1974, see Appendix E).

In his speech to the United Nations General Assembly on 13 November 1974, Arafat again gave primacy to the armed struggle, when he said: 'Even as today we address this General Assembly . . . we are expressing our faith in political and diplomatic struggle as complements, as enhancement of armed struggle' (*Journal of Palestine Studies*, Vol. 4, No. 2, Winter 1975, p. 183).

Thus the primacy of the armed struggle is a central and permanent tenet in PLO thinking. The 13th PNC (March 1977) declared (Article 2): 'The PNC affirms the stand of the PLO and its determination to continue the armed struggle, and its concomitant forms of political and mass struggle to achieve our inalienable rights.' The new element of 'mass struggle' refers to civil protest in the occupied territories. The importance of this mode of action grew as Fedayeen military action ebbed very significantly in recent years, since the borders of Jordan and Lebanon can no longer be used for incursions into Israel.

The political course of action is important only if it leads to the weakening of Israel, provided however that it does not block the possibility of achieving the final goal of the liquidation of Israel's existence, which cannot be attained by political means. The PLO expects that the Arab states which are at present applying pressure on it to moderate its stand in order to pave the way for PLO's participation in the Geneva Conference, will ultimately realise that their hopes for a political settlement in Geneva will be disappointed and that they then will revert to military means, the road of 'armed struggle.' As long as the political settlement remains on the agenda, the PLO is subject to pressure and it must resign itself to an inferior position whereas the return to a war mood improves its stance. Thus the political road in its view is only a kind of by-pass that returns to the main highway of war, as the logical outcome of the confrontation, in which, as it believes, there is no compromise.

Article 10
Commando action constitutes the nucleus of the Palestinian popular liberation war. This requires its escalation, comprehensiveness and the mobilisation of all the Palestinian popular and educational efforts and their organisation and involvement in the armed Palestinian revolution. It also requires the achieving of unity for the national (watanī) struggle among the different groupings of the Palestinian people, and between the Palestinian people and the Arab masses so as to secure the continuation of the revolution, its escalation and victory.

This article is new and describes the esoterics of Fedayeenism, how its operation and network is to expand until the entire people is engaged in its activities. The war is termed popular in view of both its goal and the wide public participation in it. A primary source of support for the Palestinians lies in the Arab people, not their governments. According to Fatah's description, this popular support constitutes the 'Supporting Arab Front.' In addition to its role in providing direct help, it must ensure that the Arab countries do not deviate from their commitments to support the 'Palestinian revolution' because of local interests or pressures. The importance of these allied popular circles increased in the PLO's eyes after the Fedayeen were routed in Jordan in September 1970. The lesson that the PLO learned was that its suppression in Jordan was possible in the absence of allies among the Jordanian masses, whom the PLO had to foster by appealing to the people over the heads of their rulers. In November 1972, a first congress of non-governmental organisations and parties supporting the Fedayeen was held in Beirut under the leadership of Kamal Junblat (a Druze leader of leftish leanings who became the leader of the left in the Lebanese war of 1976 and was assassinated in March 1977). It was called 'the Participating Arab Front.' This change of name in the Front from 'supporting' to 'participating' was meant to stress the importance of its contribution.

This approach, which regards the peoples and not the governments as the 'strategic' allies of the Palestinians is reflected in Palestinian literature, in an ambivalent and suspicious attitude toward Arab governments. The support of the Arab establishments may turn out to be tactical and volatile. It reflects awareness that contradictions lurk between the PLO and the Arab states that might break out and lead to an open rift between the PLO and the host governments. Psychologically it may be gratifying for PLO circles to believe that the Arab peoples are the real supporters of the PLO, as governments come and go while the peoples are permanent. Nevertheless, it is doubtful whether the description of the Arab people being much more loyal to the Palestinian cause than their governments is indeed accurate. It may turn out to be only wishful thinking.

Whereas in the Covenant the supporters of the Palestinian struggle are called 'the Arab masses,' after 1970 their supporters and partners are named 'the national forces,' 'the liberation forces,' 'the forces of the Arab revolution' or 'the progressive forces.' The influence of radical-wing thinking is evident here, as it claimed that the PLO could not rely on reactionaries, whose help may prove to be temporary and that it must base itself on progressive circles and regard itself as part of the 'Arab revolution.' Only these forces are its 'strategic allies.' The recommendations of the 'Participating Arab Front Committee' in the popular congress that preceded the 10th PNC (April 1972) made it clear: '. . . evidently the existence of the resistance movement and its use of any Arab country as place of departure [for its operations against Israel, Y.H.] is predicated on its protection by the national forces. The scope of the existence of the power of the national (*watanī*) resistance movement is dependent, in the last resort, on the size of the national (*watanī*) forces themselves and the extent of the protection they can provide it. Disregard of this fact and a quest after reactionary forces under the slogan of their neutralisation or other slogans is nothing but tactics of one phase that will come to an end the moment these forces consider that the Palestinian struggle develops more than they feel necessary, or beyond the point they desire' (PLO, The official report in Arabic, *The Popular Congress and PNC the Tenth Extraordinary Session, April 6–12, 1972*, p. 128–9).

The link between the Arab masses and the revolutionary circles on the one hand and the PLO on the other becomes two-way. Thus the Political Programme passed at the 11th PNC calls on the PLO to achieve 'solidarity with the Arab patriotic and progressive militants against persecution which touches their means of livelihood or touches them either physically, politically or intellectually' (*Palestine Lives*, p. 167). In other words, the PLO is required not only to seek protection from these circles but to defend them. Indeed, this contradicts the PLO's previous undertaking to refrain from interfering in the internal affairs of the Arab states, as required by Article 27 of the Covenant. The PLO's commitment to the left has already had damaging results as it was a main factor in embroiling the PLO in the war in Lebanon.

It should also be noted that the possibility of a political settlement between Israel and the Arab states has constantly worried the PLO. Therefore, the Arab masses are the trustees who will ensure that the Palestinians are not neglected nor abandoned and that they will be provided with the conditions and facilities to continue their struggle (see below, the commentary to Article 14).

Article 11
The Palestinians will have three mottoes: national (wataniyya) unity, national (qawmiyya) mobilsiation and liberation.

These slogans appear on the PLO emblems. It is worthwhile

noting that 'unity' is *watanī*, i.e., internally-Palestinian, whereas 'mobilisation' applies to all the Arab efforts on behalf of liberation. This article was copied directly from the previous version. The national unity of the Palestinians has been a burning problem since the PLO's establishment, and in some respects it has even deteriorated since the PLO became an umbrella framework for the Fedayeen groups. Many plans have been presented to unite these Fedayeen organisations, with limited results. It was easier to produce some functional unity in setting up common institutions like WAFA—the PLO news agency— but difficult to unite their military units and make them all subservient to one unified command or merge the Fedayeen organisations themselves. Each of the main organisations preserved with tenacity its individuality as an independent organisation, militarily, administratively and ideologically. It should be noted that other historical cases like the Algerian or Vietnamese wars also started with several organisations; however, during fighting some unity was achieved by the organisations coalescing together. Such a trend is much less noticeable in the PLO. Some ephemeral Fedayeen organisations have disappeared; the main groups, however, have remained.

Article 12
The Palestinian people believe in Arab unity. In order to contribute their share toward the attainment of that objective, however, they must, at the present stage of their struggle, safeguard their Palestinian identity and develop their consciousness of that identity, and oppose any plan that may dissolve or impair it.

This article is identical with the text of the 1964 Covenant. Its reasoning is apologetical, explaining that the preservation of Palestinian distinctiveness is not a manifestation of narrow nationalism (*wataniyya*) or Palestinian patriotism but only a temporary requirement which dialectically will lead to its transcendence in pan-Arabism (*qawmiyya*). This scheme recurs in Palestinian political literature as a means of proving the Palestinians' pan-Arab national orthodoxy (see commentary on Article 1). The idea of Palestininism as a temporary phase contradicts Article 4 which portrays it as an eternal quality, which by itself may prevent its dissolution or assimilation. Plans to dissolve it refer to the different project to settle the Palestinians in Arab host countries. Thus opposition to solve the problem of the unsettled Palestinians, i.e., those still in refugee camps, despite the misery it causes by perpetuating their plight, is a nationally (Arab) commendable policy which, of course, may seem very questionable to outside observers and perhaps to history.

Article 13
Arab unity and the liberation of Palestine are two complementary objectives, the attainment of either of which facilitates the attainment of the other. Thus, Arab unity leads to the liberation of Palestine; the liberation of Palestine leads to Arab unity; and work toward the realisation of one objective proceeds side by side with work toward the realisation of the other.

The text is identical with that in the previous Covenant (Article 12). Nasser used to argue that Arab unity is a prerequisite for building up Arab strength that would enable the initiation of an all-out war against Israel. Unity is the major component in Arab military preparedness and should precede war. Using this argument Nasser justified the postponement of the war against Israel despite Arab nationalist achievements which he brandished. Fatah presented an opposite view in the slogan: 'The liberation of Palestine is the road to unity.' Fatah argued that war-like actions could be launched immediately and that the heat they generate would dissolve Arab divergencies and that furthermore Arab victory over Israel would be in the nature of a spectacular, historical event forming a critical mass that would overcome the obstacles that had so far prevented unity (as Prussia's victory over France in 1870 brought about Germany's unification). Nasser's and Fatah's conceptions constitute an antinomy—a contradiction between two apparent truths or two reasonable arguments: on the one hand there should be no war against Israel prior to the achievement of preparedness by unity; on the other hand, war is the vehicle by which unity will come. In the Covenant there is a sort of verbal compromise, evading the issue as if both events—unity and victory over Israel—could and will be achieved simultaneously.

Article 14

The destiny of the Arab nation, and indeed Arab existence itself, depends upon the destiny of the Palestine cause. From this interdependence springs the Arab nation's pursuit of, and striving for, the liberation of Palestine. The people of Palestine play the role of the vanguard in the realisation of this sacred national (qawmī) goal.

As in the previous 1964 version (Article 13), the Palestinian problem is fateful for the very existence of the Arabs as a nation. Therefore, the liberation of Palestine or the liquidation of Israel is an imperative of survival for the Arabs, as if a *force majeure* which is beyond praise or condemnation. The argumentations that are usually produced to support it are: Israel prevents all the Arabs from realising their national goals and will continue to be a focus of irritation that will distract them from their constructive effort in developing their countries. Moreover, Israel's existence will lead to her expansion and the erasure of the Arabism of further Arab regions.

The Palestinians have an interest in defining the struggle against Israel as crucial and central for all Arab states in order to spur them on to activity. Perhaps this formula also hides a tendency to portray the conflict as symmetrical—as if both sides were threatening each other with extermination, and thus survival is at stake for both Israel and the Arab world.

The case can be made that what really is at stake is Israel's survival versus Arab grandeur, if one assumes, and this is questionable, that the failure of the Arabs to bring about Israel's demise would tarnish their grandeur. Herein lies the basic asymmetry in the conflict. Possibly, the Arabs may assume that grandeur is a necessary condition for their existence; this may seem to outside observers as arbitrary and even objectionable.

Both in this and the following article, a formula is presented for a division of labour: in the fighting, the Palestinians will be the vanguard leading the Arab camp, yet their mission is on behalf of pan-Arabism. Such a division implies too a demand that the Palestinians shall not only lead but direct the struggle and that the rest shall resign themselves to the role of following suit.

Articles 14 and 15 attempt to lay down that the Arab states have no more important goals than the struggle against Israel. The duty of aiding the Palestinians is presented as overriding every other national interest; hence, the demand that the Palestinians be aided in their struggle without reservations. However, what will happen if there is a conflict with other aims and interests of the Arab states that demand resources and claim attention? Would they really be ready to sacrifice everything on the altar of the conflict? The Covenant solves the problem verbally; it is enough to point out that the Palestinian question is crucial, and this will induce the Arabs to give it supreme priority and devote their resources to it.

Nevertheless, expressions of suspicion of and ambivalence toward the Arab states abound in Palestinian writings. They contain sharp criticism of discrimination against the Palestinians in the form of restrictive decrees in employment and travel. Expressions of hatred can even be found against the Arab states, and also complaints that the Arab leaders have used the Palestinians in their political maneuvers in inter-Arab rivalries and in the dispute with Israel, without regard for Palestinian interests. Suspicion is repeatedly expressed that the Arab states may eventually abandon the Palestinians and conclude peace with Israel.

It is not accidental that an important document such as the Covenant, which by its very nature is limited and economical in phrasing, devotes three articles (10, 14 and 15) to the relationship between the Arabs and the Palestinians and the support the latter should be given. It proves the importance of the topic. It is worthwhile examining what each article adds to this matter. In Article 10, the Palestinians pin their hopes on popular support. Article 14 discusses the matter on the national level and Article 15 deals with the governmental level. These articles follow Articles 12 and 13, which discuss the opposite direction—the Palestinian contribution to the Arabs. Furthermore, Articles 27 and 28 deal with another aspect of Arab and Palestinian relationship, i.e., the principle of respective non-interference.

The pretension that the needs of the struggle against Israel overshadow all other Arab interests and goals has led the Palestinians to demand excessive freedom for their activities in the Arab countries, even if these operations ran counter to local interests and infringed on the sovereignty of these states. This led them into open conflicts with the Arab states, such as Jordan in September 1970 and Lebanon in 1976.

Furthermore, in the very assertion that the Palestinian problem is fateful for all Arabs lurks a paradox, because if the issué is so important, then the Arab states cannot abdicate and leave all decisions on the conflict in the hands of the Palestinians, acquiescing in advance in all that the PLO might do (see Article 29). The very assertion of fatefulness invites intervention by the Arab states and thus the ruling that the problem is fateful for the Arabs may become fateful and dangerous for the PLO itself. The PLO's assertion that 'what is good for the PLO is good for the Arabs' may encounter similar claims by Egypt and Syria that what is good for their country is good for the Arabs and Palestinians, or the pretensions of Jordan that the preservation of its existence is of pan-Arab, and not only Jordanian, interest.

The liberation of Palestine assumes another dimension of importance, besides the national one, as crucial for the Arab success in achieving social revolution. Examining the terminology employed in PNC resolutions, a trend toward the use of leftist jargon is noticeable. It marked a rise in the influence of the PLO radical wing. The resolutions of the 10th PNC (which started as a Popular Congress with broader participation) and the 11th PNC in which the ideas of both meetings were crystallised in the 'PLO Political Programme' bear this out.

The 'PLO Political Programme' decreed: 'The struggle for the realisation of the Arab national democratic revolution will be neither unified nor deepened nor will it broaden and succeed in achieving its purpose, except by liquidating the Zionist imperialist base which aims at its very foundations' (*Palestine Lives*, p. 166). 'Democratic' stands here for internal or social as the elimination of special privileges of the higher classes, on the road to social egalitarianism and democracy. Thus winning the Arab–Israeli conflict is described as a necessary condition for the Arabs achieving both their national and social objectives.

In PFLP thinking the heat that the conflict generates will revolutionise the Arab world and ensure the success of the social revolutions, which in their term will homogenise the Arab world, thus enabling its unification. Unity will then produce the necessary conglomeration of power to defeat Israel and liquidate its national existence. In this historical scheme the conflict enters twice: at the beginning and at the end.

Article 15

The liberation of Palestine, from an Arab viewpoint, is a national (qawmī) duty and it attempts to repel the Zionist and Imperialist aggression against the Arab homeland, and aims at the elimination of Zionism in Palestine. Absolute responsibility for this falls upon the Arab nation—peoples and governments—with the Arab people of Palestine in the vanguard. Accordingly, the Arab nation must mobise all its military, human, moral and spiritual capabilities to participate actively with the Palestinian people in the liberation of Palestine. It must, particularly in the phase of the armed Palestinian revolution, offer and furnish the Palestinian people with all possible help, and material and human support, and make available to them the means and opportunities that will enable them to continue to carry out their leading role in the armed revolution, until they liberate their homeland.

The change in this article as compared with the earlier version (Article 14) lies mainly in the stress on the 'active participation' of the Arab states. It may imply a concern that without the support of the Arab states the 'Palestinian revolution' may lose its momentum. Thus the final responsibility for the struggle is pan-Arab. The aim of the struggle against Israel is two-fold: defense of the Arab countries and the expulsion of Zionism from Palestine. 'The elimination of Zionism in Palestine' does not mean that Israel shall cease to be Zionist, but that Israel as the embodiment of Zionism shall cease to exist on Palestinian territory.

Article 16

The liberation of Palestine, from a spiritual point of view, will provide the Holy Land with an atmosphere of safety and tranquillity, which in turn will safeguard the country's religious sanctuaries and guarantee freedom of worship and of visit to all, without discrimination of race, colour, language, or religion. Accordingly, the people of Palestine look to all spiritual forces in the world for support.

There is hardly any change here from the wording of the earlier version (Article 15). The 'visit' means pilgrimage to the Holy Places. This and the following articles describe the benefits that will accrue from the liquidation of Israel, not only to the Palestinians but to international society. Earlier on, the liquidation of Israel was the outcome of definitions of essence; here the approach is utilitarian—commencing with the spiritual and religious beneficial results and the convenience for pilgrimage.

Article 17

The liberation of Palestine, from a human point of view, will restore to the Palestinian individual his dignity, pride and freedom. Accordingly, the Palestinian Arab people look forward to the support of all those who believe in the dignity of man and his freedom in the world.

The scope of utility shifts to the Palestinian person. The very existence of Israel and the lack of a homeland creates alienation in the Palestinian individual. He is thereby deprived of his dignity and is placed in a state of bondage; his life is 'not normal' (Article 9). As long as the State of Israel exists, the Palestinian has a defective truncated personality. This article is a new addition reflecting Fatah thinking, and the influence of modern revolutionary literature, such as the writing of Frantz Fanon (see the author's *Fedayeen Action and Arab Strategy*, p. 14).

Article 18

The liberation of Palestine, from an international point of view, is a defensive action necessitated by the demands of self-defence. Accordingly, the Palestinian people, desirous as they are of the friendship of all people, look to freedom-loving, justice-loving and peace-loving states for support in order to restore their legitimate rights in Palestine, to re-establish peace and security in the country, and to enable its people to exercise national sovereignty and freedom.

The article is almost identical with that of the previous Covenant (Article 16). It summarises typical Arab legalistic argumentations. The liquidation of Israel is legitimate because her existence is illegal; she represents a 'permanent illegality' or 'a phenomenon of juridical pathology' (Seminar of Arab jurists on Palestine, *The Palestine Question*, p. 91). The demand for the demise of Israel is not contrary to international law but follows from it. Aggression against Israel is not aggressive but is lawful as merely thwarting of aggression, exercising self-defence. It is frequently claimed in Palestinian literature that the assault of the Fedayeen on Israel is legal and stems from the right to self-determination and national liberation, while Israel's defensive measures, and even more so its retaliatory attacks, are illegal because their aim is to perpetuate the state that embodies aggression by its very establishment and its continued existence. An example of this is the article of Ibrahim al-'Abid, 'The Causes of the Last Israeli Aggression' (the Six Day War), in which he wrote: 'Fedayeen action is one of the rights of the Palestinian people, because the right of national liberation is an extension of the right of peoples to self-defence, a right that has been approved by the UN charter as a natural and original right' (Anis Sayegh, *Filastiniyat* (Palestinian issues), p. 107).

Article 19
The partition of Palestine in 1947 and the establishment of the State of Israel are entirely illegal, regardless of the passage of time, because they were contrary to the will of the Palestinian people and to their natural right in their homeland, and inconsistent with the principles embodied in the Charter of the United Nations, particularly the right to self-determination.

This article is identical with the version in the earlier Covenant (Article 17). This and the following Article 20 continue the preceding article in explaining the illegality of the existence of Israel. This legalistic offensive goes on from attacking the enactments of a later period (1947) to attacking, in the following article, the earlier enactments of 1917 and their historical justification. The UN Partition Resolution has no legal validity as expressing an international enactment that granted Israel legitimacy and embodied supreme international recognition, for several reasons. Firstly, it violated the 'will' of the Palestinian people. This assertion arbitrarily demands world acceptance of the illegality of a phenomenon simply on the basis that it was not wanted.

Secondly, the Partition Resolution contradicts a 'natural right' of the Palestinians. This claim too is pretentious. A 'natural right' derives from the 'law of nature,' as the gist of basic rules that every person recognises. Whoever repudiates them is supposedly contradicting his human nature. A natural right, according to the doctrine of 'the law of nature,' precedes any legal recognition based on it. The Partition Resolution is a legislation, 'positive law,' but it lacks validity as it contradicts the law of nature, which is divine legislation.

Thirdly, the Partition Resolution is described as a deviation from positive international law, by contradicting a basic principle: the right of self-determination in the UN Charter is revealed in Article 103 which lays down that in case an obligation stemming from the Charter conflicts with any other international obligation the former shall prevail.

According to the Palestinians' definition, the realisation of their right of self-determination is conditional on the liquidation of Israel. Self-determination for both Palestinians and Israelis is excluded, even proscribed.

In Palestinian political literature the idea that the very existence of Israel rules out Palestinian self-determination is repeatedly put forward. For instance, Ibrahim al-'Abid, in his book *A Guide to the Palestinian Problem* (in Arabic), states: 'Israel exists, because there is no Palestine. The Israelis are situated in the place of the Palestinians, because the Palestinians are not where they should be found, i.e., in the land of their forefathers, but live in exile. The very existence of Israel is an act that leads to the non-existence and abolition of Palestine and its original inhabitants; the very existence of Israel means: non-recognition of the Palestinian people and its authentic right to live in its land and enjoy its rights to self-determination over its homeland' (p. 224–5).

The political platform submitted by the Political Committee to the Popular Palestinian Congress that preceded the 10th Council (April 1972) stated: 'The right of self-determination in relation to the Palestinian people means [its right] to the liberation of the entire homeland and the establishment of a Palestinian national state in it. This is the meaning of the right to self-determination scientifically and legally' (PLO, *The Popular Congress and PNC, the 10th Session,* p. 105). Palestinian self-determination is the right to have an Arab nation-state over the whole territory of Palestine. The Palestinian right of self-determination is thus also a euphemistic expression for the liquidation of Israel.

Article 20
The Balfour Declaration, the Mandate for Palestine and everything that has been based upon them, are deemed null and void. Claims of historical or religious ties of Jews with Palestine are incompatible with the facts of history and the true conception of what constitutes statehood. Judaism being a divine religion is not an independent nationality. Nor do Jews constitute a single nation with an identity of its own: they are citizens of the states to which they belong.

This article is identical with the earlier 1964 version. The Shuqairy draft contained the following phrase after Judaism—'a divine religion worthy of esteem and respect,' which was deleted.

This article contains the legal undermining of the antecedents to Israel. The Balfour Declaration and the Mandate, ratified by the League of Nations, are invalidated high-handedly. The reasons evidently follow from the previous article. But as both documents were based on a recognition of the Jewish historical link to Palestine, the refutation of such a relationship is the main thrust of the article. Some of the principal arguments in Arab political writing that have been presented to this effect are: the ancient Jews lived for only a short period in the country; their exclusive rule in the kingdom of David and Solomon was brief and generally their partners were Canaanite tribes, whom modern Arab historiography considers ancient Arabs; Arab residence in the country has been longer than that of the Jews; they did not conquer the land from the Jews and therefore do not have to return it to them. Sometimes, it is argued that even if the promise of God to Abraham indeed referred to his seed, which would multiply as the stars in the skies and the sand upon the seashore, this means that Abraham's seed should also include the Arabs and the Christians, since the Jews are not so numerous. This article goes much further, even denying the historical links of the Jews with Palestine. The claim of the Palestinians to exclusive rights over Palestine leads to the absolutist position of denying any similar rights to the Jews.

Another argument is evoked: the modern state is an expression of the principle of nationalism and not religion. Thus the Jews, who are here referred to as constituting a religious group, do not need a state at all. Thus Zionism that has turned Judaism into nationalism perverts the very nature of Judaism. The modern state is built on the separation of religion and state, whereas Zionism anachronistically fuses the two. Therefore, the state of Israel is an anachronistic and depraved state. It should be stressed that this is a strange argument coming particularly from the Arabs, as most Arab constitutions proclaim Islam as the state religion or Muslim religious law as the source of legislation.

The apparent conclusion to be drawn from the argument in this article is that instead of demanding a national state of their own, the Jews should become assimilated in their countries of residence. Even the Israeli Jews do not constitute, after the establishment of the state, a national group. The Israeli Jews, as Jews in general, are of an inferior status or nature. They can only be *natives* of states, whose nationality is not Jewish.

The demand for the liquidation of Israel thus also stems directly as a necessary conclusion from the definition that the Jews are not a nation. Nāji 'Alūsh criticised the inconsistency of communism vis-à-vis Israel, when he wrote: '. . . subsequently, communism refused to recognise the Jews as a nation, without uttering the motto that this stand implied, i.e., the liquidation of the State of Israel' (*The Road to Palestine*, p. 141).

Since the State of Israel is not based on true nationalism, it is often described in Arabic as an 'artificial entity.' This is also presented as evidence that Israel's power is transient and that it can be liquidated. In Fedayeen literature this argument is put forward as proof that acts of subversion will lead to an erosion of the cohesion of the Israelis, until they agree to relinquish their Jewish statehood.

The theory that the Jews do not constitute a nation is also required for the claim of exclusive Arab nationality of the democratic Palestinian state. Even if the Israeli Jews remain in it in large numbers, its Arab national character will not be diluted by a group that lacks national traits but will be stamped by that sector of the population that possesses a national nature, i.e., the Arab alone.

This article, like Article 6, makes no reference to *Israeli* Jews, but to Jews in general. In 1917 no 'Israeli people' existed and the Jews in it were only Jews; in 1968, however, the Israelis formed a people or a nation. As far as the Palestinians are concerned, the Covenant stipulates that they are a 'Palestinian Arab people' and indeed the Israelis too are the 'Israeli-Jewish people.' However, admission of the Israeliness of the Israelis would have meant recognition of another bond they shared beyond religion, as a manifestation of nationalism.

The Covenant refutes the very right of Israel to exist on three grounds:

1. The Palestinian right is put forward as possessing axiomatic validity.
2. Israel by its nature is a non-state, because the Israelis as Jews do not constitute a political community. This is an attack on Israel from within.
3. From the outside, the existence of Israel is illegal, because it is a manifestation of a political, aberrant phenomenon.

Article 21

The Arab Palestinian people, expressing themselves by the armed Palestinian revolution, reject all solutions which are substituting for the total liberation of Palestine and reject all proposals aiming at the liquidation of the Palestinian problem, or its internationalisation.

This article is new. It refers to the problems that arose after the Six Day War, in particular, the Security Council Resolution 242. It is an almost verbatim repetition of an article in the charter of the Fedayeen organisations which met in Cairo in January 1968 under Fatah initiative which stated: 'All solutions intended to serve as a substitute for the liquidation of the occupying Zionist entity in Palestine must be rejected, and so are rejected all programmes designed to liquidate the Palestinian problem or its internationalisation or impose tutelage on our people whatever is their source' (*Fatah Yearbook 1968*, p. 128). This is one of the most important articles in the 1968 Covenant. It wraps up the complications for an 'absolutist-totalistic' stand when encountering circumstances calling for a political course of action. In order to explain this issue we have to examine the evolution of Arab thinking.

The previous prevailing Arab stand, which had been given prominence by Nasser, was that the liquidation of Israel would come about through an all-out war. There was a certain logic in linking the liquidation of Israel and war; the wiping out of a state must occur through a spectacular historical *event* such as war. A political procedure is not compatible with the realisation of such an absolute objective, since it involves mutual concessions and compromises and no state would consent to be liquidated. The gravity of the political goal led to the rejection of a gradualist approach in which the aim is achieved by a *process*, step-by-step, *incrementally*. A proposal for achieving the goal by political means incrementally was raised by the Tunisian President Bourguiba in 1965. He argued that Israel's technological superiority made it impossible to defeat her in war and thus war could not serve the Arabs. He proposed that the Arabs declare their readiness to make peace with Israel, if she withdrew to the Partition Resolution borders of 29 November 1947. If Israel consented, she would be weakened, and that might help the Arab in due course when the final solution of the conflict was on the agenda. That is to say, after Israel's withdrawal there would be further stages of Arab pressure which Bourguiba did not spell out. If Israel refused, the Arabs would have gained an advantage diplomatically by showing that they were ready for a compromise and peace according to UN resolutions. Bourguiba's proposal evoked sharp reactions against him in the Arab states and particularly in PLO circles. The main charge levelled against him was that his plan would fail to achieve the Arab objective and that even if this was not his intention, it would lead to the perpetuation of Israel's existence even if in smaller dimensions.

Nasser rejected the incremental idea in its military version too, in other words the beginning of hostilities against Israel in the form of border incursions and a limited war, as proposed by Syria. He argued that Israel might exploit her military superiority and escalate the limited operations initiated by the Arabs and turn them into an overall war and a crushing defeat for the Arabs. The Arabs could afford to start a war only when they were fully ready—by achieving preponderant superiority over Israel, which is needed to defeat Israel in a short war, before the West intervened to protect her. The attainment of such superiority was a long process that demanded social, economic and political transformations in Arab society. Nasser was thus enmeshed in a contradiction: he advocated an all-out war, thereby displaying extremism; nevertheless, he postponed the war to a distant future—-this manifested moderation; thus, adherence to the objective of destroying Israel was coupled with restraint and realism in the very recognition that it was unfeasible in the near future.

Nasser's linking liquidation and an all-out war had the merit of internal consistency. Its weakness was practical--the long delay needed for attaining military superiority. Another disadvantage was political as this conception made no bones about the deadly gravity of the Arab objective.

The Fedayeen proposed another course of action to overcome the practical difficulty of attaining supremacy and the need for delay, by starting a guerrilla war forthwith in which Israel's existence would be nibbled away. Such a plan would also enable the evasion of the political difficulty, since the goal was presented as a war of liberation of an oppressed and weak people against an oppressing state. However, the very meagre achievements of the Fedayeen in guerrilla warfare proved the inefficiency of their method.

The Six Day War served as decisive proof that Bourguiba had been right in arguing that the Arabs would be defeated in war and that it could not serve them as an instrument for attaining their objectives. Furthermore, the war placed the Arabs in a grave dilemma for, in order to regain the territories they had lost, they had to pay the high price of consent to Security Council Resolution 242, which deviated from the fundamental Arab objective of liquidating Israel by demanding recognition of secure and agreed borders for all states of the region. The PLO bitterly rejected Resolution 242, regarding it as a flagrant contradiction of its objectives.

The 4th Council detailed the reasons for the rejection of this resolution: it would end the state of hostility; ensure freedom of navigation; terminate the boycott; relax economic pressure on Israel; ensure trade relations; guarantee secure borders includ-

ing a *de facto* recognition of Israel; besides, it was 'an encroach-
ment on the unconditional right of the Palestinian Arab people
to the whole of Palestine.' It would also entail an end to the
Palestinian revolution; a ban on Fedayeen operations; the
establishment of peace, which would lead to increased immigration to Israel. An obstacle to immigration and in particular of
Soviet Jewry would disappear; so would the factor that prevented recognition of Israel by foreign countries; a geographical
barrier would be established between the eastern and western
Arab world; it would be a blow to the Palestinian armed
struggle; the Arab liberation movement would suffer; imperialistic influence in the Arab world would increase; the Arabs
would have to abandon the policy of neutrality; the resolution
ignored the political rights of the Palestinians to their homeland
by referring to them as a refugee problem; Arab dignity would
be harmed; and the resolution might give the Arabs a false sense
of security against Israel's subsequent expansionism (*International Documents on Palestine, 1968*, p. 402–03).

The 4th Council also angrily rejected the idea of establishing
a Palestinian state in the West Bank, reiterating that its establishment would be 'an act that totally contradicted the right of the
Palestinian-Arab people to all of its homeland.' It termed such
a state an *'amil*—satellite state—and threatened that any
individual or group calling for the establishment of such a state
would be considered an enemy of the Palestinian people and
the Arab nation (p. 40 in the original Arabic report of the 4th
PNC).

The central idea of the PLO that the goal must be totally
achieved contradicts any possibility of a compromise solution,
which must by its very nature be a partial solution and a
substitute for obtaining the entire goal. Any solution less than
'complete liberation' is denounced in PLO language as the
'liquidation' of the Palestinian problem. An Israel of any size is
depicted as a total defeat of Arabism. Victory for the Arabs is
possible only in the liquidation of Israel; anything else is
capitulation. Any partial settlement, even if intended to be
provisional, until further pressure is exerted on Israel to shrink
in size, may backfire; a partial settlement may lead to a freezing
of the problem, i.e., perpetuation of the existence of a small
Israel.

The agreement of 6 May 1970, states (Article 7): 'The people of Palestine and their national liberation movement are struggling for complete liberation and reject all peaceful solutions involving liquidation and surrender including reactionary and colonialist conspiracies to establish a Palestinian state in part of Palestinian territory and the resolution involving liquidation adopted by the Security Council Resolution of 22 November 1967' (*International Documents on Palestine, 1970,* p. 795).

The rejection of a political solution, including the establishment of a Palestinian state in the West Bank, has been a permanent topic at all the Palestinian Councils since then. Its very repetition in PNC resolutions indicates that it is not a one-time, marginal matter, but a central tenet and doctrine. The vehemence of the rejection of such a solution and its denunciation not only express the depth of opposition to the idea, but also the concern that it might materialise. The PLO Political Programme approved by the 11th Council (January 1973) not only opposed a Palestinian state but expressed its abhorrence at the 'compromising mentality' from which such a sacrilegious idea may rise; they vowed 'To militate against the compromising mentality and the plans it spawns which are either contrary to our people's cause of national liberation or aim to liquidate this cause through "proposed Palestinian states" or through a Palestinian state on part of the Palestinian natural soil' (*Palestine Lives,* p. 162). It implied too the disgust felt by a movement boasting to be revolutionary towards a political solution lacking in vigour and stigmatised as reformist.

For their part, the Arab states understood that without deviating from the goal of absolute liquidation of Israel, they could not recover their territories, and that the 'removal of the traces of the 1967 aggression' required some apparent concession, even regarding the goal of 'removing the traces of the 1948 aggression.' The Arabs attempted to persuade the PLO that it had nothing to fear, because a way would be found to continue the struggle for the attainment of the final goal even after the areas were returned and a peace agreement signed between the Arab states and Israel. Any such agreement would not end the conflict but would merely create an armistice and a pause leading to a renewal of the struggle in better circumstances. Acceptance of a solution would only be a temporary stage in an incremental process. The Arabs would thus refuse to undertake a final commitment to coexist with Israel and see to it that it would be an open-ended peace without the concrete essence of peaceful relations. It was also claimed that the 'removal of the traces of the 1967 aggression' was a condition and preamble for 'removing the traces of the 1948 aggression.' Furthermore Israel's withdrawal according to Resolution 242 would cause a grave crisis within Israeli society; its people would lose faith in the future of the state; and a process of internal disintegration would commence, leading to the state's withering away. Thus Resolution 242 which was meant to ensure the existence of all the states in the Middle East would become for Israel by a dialectical development not an assurance of safety but a means of destruction—the whole process is termed in Arabic 'phased strategy.'

The 'internationalisation' in the text of the article alludes to a proposal that was put forward to place the West Bank under UN tutelage for several years and hold a referendum, in which the inhabitants would express their will—either to return to Jordanian rule or establish an independent state.

The Yom Kippur War served as proof that a limited war is a viable means that the Arabs can employ, because in contrast to Nasser's forebodings, the intervention of the powers turned out to be not against the Arabs but in their favour—imposing a ceasefire which saved them from defeat. Thus a joint political and military path opened up before the Arabs to pressure Israel to contract in size by returning the territories she had captured in 1967.

Acceptance by several Arab states of Resolution 242 in the form in which Resolution 338 referred to it, once again raised the problem for the Palestinians of their isolation. They faced a direct threat: refusal to participate in the political process might lead to the West Bank being returned to Jordan, should the Geneva conference be held in the absence of the Palestinians because of their rejection of both Resolution 242 and a West Bank Palestinian state.

At the 12th PNC (June 1974) and even earlier, a lengthy debate was held on these issues. As a result, a sophisticated compromise resolution was passed.

The total rejection of Resolution 242 was toned down, as it

were, as though it was not the entire resolution that was objectionable, but one aspect of it only, i.e., that it ignored all the national rights (*wataniyya*) and pan-nationalism (*qawmiyya*) of the Palestinians and referred to their problem merely as a refugee one. The linking of their rights with both categories of nationalism is meant to stress that Palestinian rights do not exist only in a narrow Palestinian framework but in a broad inter-Arab context, which should be given expression in the settlement, i.e., Palestine as an integral part of the Arab homeland.

The compromise adopted stipulated that 'the Liberation Organisation will employ all means, and first and foremost the armed struggle, to liberate the Palestinian territory and to establish the independent national combatant for the people over every part of Palestinian territory that is liberated' (see Appendix E, Article 2). The expression 'every part' etc. apparently is meant to describe a continuous incremental process of Israel's contraction. This resolution implied consent to a Palestinian state on the West Bank, which was hedged by a reservation which seemingly turned everything upside down, as further on Article 3 stated: 'The Liberation Organisation will struggle against any proposal for a Palestinian entity at the price of recognition, peace, secure frontiers, renunciation of national rights and the deprival of our people of their right of return and their right to self-determination on the soil of their homeland' (*ibid.*) .In other words, consent to a state on the West Bank was dependent on the assurance that irredentism—the claim to the entire Israeli territory—would be preserved. The old strategic objective of removing Israel remained valid and the acceptance of a Palestinian state on the West Bank would be a tactical, interim stage, in the framework of an incremental, open-ended version of this phased strategy.

These articles thus formulated imply that agreement to a state on the West Bank does not mean a final settlement, or a solution that would suspend or freeze the continuation of the struggle or repudiate the final Palestinian goal. The struggle would go on.

PLO opposition to interim settlements between the Arab states and Israel is limited to settlements that entail a delayed or muzzled incrementality which may end belligerency and terminate the conflict. Nevertheless, the question remains open whether such a continuous incrementality can be embodied in any political agreement; can Israel agree to be a party to an agreement that leaves open the possibility of the struggle against her going on? Would not Israeli opposition to such a *sham* political settlement gain international support? These very questions beset the PLO. The Rejection Front's main argument is that a settlement which leaves open the door to incrementality is a contradiction in terms and that the Arabs will be forced of necessity to terminate the conflict. Therefore it rejects any political settlement.

Despite all these drawbacks, it should be noted that the wording of the resolution of the 12th Council provided a propaganda advantage from the Arab viewpoint. This text removed to some extent the character of 'absolutism' from the Arab and Palestinian stand and made it more relative. People could be led to believe or interpret Palestinian readiness to accept a state on the West Bank as showing incipient readiness to coexist with Israel, even if nothing was further from the truth. This enabled government circles and world public opinion to get round the need of rejecting the absolutism of the Arab stand.

The resolution of the 12th Council did not call the state on the West Bank 'state' or 'a government,' but *sulta*—an authority. Presumably this term was chosen as a semantic device for mellowing the open contradiction with the previous consistent PLO stand that so emphatically ruled out a state on the West Bank. The term 'state' might also indicate a final, complete entity, while 'an authority' could be regarded as a provisional affair. Moreover, a state is bound to keep international commitments, while a revolutionary body claims to be free of them. However, it should be noted that this distinction between a state and an authority may be minor. In many instances in Arab political publications the Palestinian entity in the West Bank has been called a state and the resolutions of the 13th Council called it so explicitly.

A further development on this issue took place at the 13th PNC (March 1977). Since the 12th Council, the status of the PLO had improved in the international arena, primarily due to General Assembly Resolution 3236 of 22 November 1974, which recognized the rights of the Palestinian people to self-determination, sovereignty and national independence and to return to their homes, as well as its right to restore its rights by all means. This resolution recognised that the Palestinians are a principal party in a settlement of the Palestine question and instructed the Secretary-General to establish contact with the PLO on all matters concerning the problem of Palestine. The 13th Council continued the line of rejection of Resolution 242 (Articles 1 and 4; see Appendix F), but demanded the right of the PLO to participate in every international conference on the conflict by the authority of Resolution 3236. It should be stressed that the 13th PNC resolutions do not signify at all a change in the PLO's traditional position of rejection of a political compromise solution, but only a demand to participate in any conference dealing with the conflict.

Article 22

Zionism is a political movement organically associated with international imperialism and antagonistic to all action for liberation and to progressive movements in the world. It is racist and fanatic in its nature, aggressive, expansionist and colonialist in its aims, and fascist in its methods. Israel is the instrument of the Zionist movement, and a geographical base for world imperialism placed strategically in the midst of the Arab homeland to combat the hopes of the Arab nation for liberation, unity and progress.

In comparison with the old version (Article 19), the new text contains a stronger denunciation of Zionism and Israel by stressing their links with imperialism. The Arab struggle against Israel is not only political but ideological. Ideologizing a conflict makes it harsher as the dispute does not revolve merely around material assets which are divisible and thus allow for a compromise. Elevating the conflict as a dispute on ideas and values, good and evil, makes a compromise extremely arduous.

Zionism is the basic cause of the conflict and a source of evil; it is the incarnated spirit of imperialism which symbolises immorality and covetousness in the international arena and serves as imperialism's agent and tool. This relationship between Zionism and imperialism is inherent as part of their makeup and thus immutable. Zionism is a pathological phenomenon as the nationalism of a non-nation, as Article 20 characterises the Jews, which causes it to be a conglomeration of vice. The abject characteristics of Zionism are paraded in this article with momentum and vehemence that is meant to reinforce the impression that Zionism is indeed an absolute evil. The catalogue of odium is so exhaustive that nothing imaginable can be politically more despicable. Zionism, it says, is a 'political movement,' it even lacks a spiritual basis. (For an explanation of this emphasis see the author's *Arab Attitudes to Israel*, Chapter 4, and the list of denunciations of Zionism detailed in it.) The conflict is thus polarised between one side that is totally depraved and unjust and the other, good and right that only fell victim to wickedness.

This Manichean division between good and evil was expressed by the resolutions of the 4th Council in these words: 'The hallmark of Palestinian Arab people is resistance, struggle and liberation, that of the enemy aggression, usurpation, the disavowal of all values governing decent, human relations' (*International Documents on Palestine, 1968*, p. 400). The evil in Israel does not merely reside in what she has committed against the Arabs, but in her very existence. The condemnation of Zionism is designed to undermine the moral basis of Israel's existence. A decent Israel is a contradiction in terms and hence, it is not adequate to correct some blemishes in Israel but to abolish it altogether.

Such an extreme portrayal of the enemy may also serve the purpose of dehumanising him, excluding him from the pale of humanity deserving compassion.

The explanation is frequently offered in Arab political literature that the West regarded the Arab renaissance as a threat to its position, and it therefore ensured the creation of Israel, charging Zionism with the mission of preventing Arab development by diverting its effort from internal construction.

This article is designed to convey that it is not the Arabs who are hostile to Israel, but Zionism that is the enemy of the Palestinians and all that is good in the world. In this way the struggle against Israel is elevated from the narrow framework of a selfish affair of the Arabs to a sublime universal mission of combating the 'enemy of humanity,' a phrase found in Arab writing to designate Israel. Such a description is designed to mobilise support from all peoples, because Zionism is portrayed as an imperialist base that threatens them too.

The second paragraph of Article 22 reads:

Israel is a constant source of threat vis-à-vis peace in the middle east and the whole world. Since the liberation of Palestine will destroy the Zionist and Imperialist presence and will contribute to the establishment of peace in the middle east, the Palestinian people look for the support of all the progressive and peaceful forces and urge them all, irrespective of their affiliations and beliefs, to offer the Palestinian people all aid and support in their just struggle for the liberation of their homeland.

The previous text was shorter and part of the preceding section:

'Israel in its capacity as a spearhead of this destructive movement and the pillar for colonialism is a permanent source of international turmoil in the Middle East in particular, and the international community in general. Because of this the people of Palestine are worthy of the support and assistance of the community of nations.'

This second half of the article describes the struggle against Israel as part of the overall battle of the forces of progress and light. The well-being of the world, not just that of the Palestinians and the Middle East, requires that Israel be liquidated. Thus, utilitarian argumentation is added to the intrinsic definition of the evil in Israel as the offspring of Zionism.

Article 23
The demands of security and peace, as well as the demands of right and justice, require all states to consider Zionism an illegitimate movement, to outlaw its existence, and to ban its operations, in order that friendly relations among peoples may be preserved, and the loyalty of citizens to their respective homelands safeguarded.

This article is identical with the previous 1964 version (Article 20). It is, in effect a practical legalistic conclusion derived from the preceding article. If Zionism is so reprehensible, its existence must be outlawed.

Considerations of morality (peace, justice and friendship) and utilitarianism (security and internal order) both require the states of the world to be hostile to Zionism.

Zionism produces political chaos and international disorder as it calls for 'dual loyalty' by Jews, i.e., loyalty to Israel alongside their loyalty to the contries in which they are citizens. Thus world order requires that it be banned.

Article 24
The Palestinian people believe in the principles of justice, freedom, sovereignty, self-determination, human dignity, and in the right of all peoples to exercise them.

The end of this article (21) in the previous Covenant is omitted: 'It also supports all international efforts to bring about peace on the basis of justice and free international cooperation.'

Juxtaposed against the evils of Israel and Zionism as claimed in the previous articles, this article praises the virtues of the Palestinians who adhere to moral values and the basic principles on which the international political order is based. These benevolent principles are applicable to all with, of course, one exception—Israel and the Israelis.

Article 22 of the 1964 Covenant, which is a continuation of the previous section, was deleted. It stated: 'The people of Palestine believe in peaceful coexistence on the basis of legal existence, for there can be no coexistence with aggression, nor can there be peace with occupation and colonialism.' This statement refers to a slogan that made its appearance at that time in the international arena concerning 'peaceful coexistence' among states, despite differences of regime and ideologies. Israel is an exception with which there can be no coexistence, since it is colonialist and aggressive. The deletion may have been due to the fact that it was repetitive.

Article 25
For the realisation of the goals of this Charter and its principles, the Palestine Liberation Organisation will perform its role in the liberation of Palestine.

This article (excluding the final phrase 'in accordance with the Constitution of this Organisation') is identical with the earlier version (Article 23). In this and the following article, the PLO is presented as an umbrella organisation, which bears the overall responsibility of all Palestinians for the struggle against Israel. The PLO is thus the operational arm of the Covenant; in the Covenant resides its *raison d'être.*

These articles, dealing with the PLO's functions, ignore an important question—the source of the PLO's legitimacy. From the inter-Arab viewpoint, the PLO's authority comes from the recognition it was granted by the second Arab summit conference that met in Alexandria in September 1964. However, neither in Shuqairy's time, nor in the subsequent period, have any elections been held in Palestinian centres. Article 5 of the PLO Constitution stated: 'The members of the National Assembly [PNC–Y.H.] shall be elected by the Palestinian people by direct ballot'; but this has never taken place. In the past, Shuqairy selected the members of the PLO's Executive Committee and appointed, or at least confirmed, the list of members of the National Councils, while after him, since the 4th PNC, members of the Councils and the Executive Committee have mostly been directly, or indirectly in the guise of independent representatives, delegates of the Fedayeen organisations. The legitimacy of the PLO is superimposed, except perhaps that the almost total lack of opposition of the Palestinians to the PLO signifies acceptance of its authority. (Paradoxically the elections held in Judea and Samaria in 1976, in which several leaders who proclaimed their allegiance to the PLO were elected, are the only ones that expressed popular recognition of the PLO.)

In the new version, Article 24 of the 1964 Covenant was deleted. It stated: 'The organisation does not exercise any regional sovereignty over the Western Bank in the Hashemite Kingdom of Jordan, on the Gaza Strip or the Hamma area. Its activities will be on the national popular level in the liberationist, organisational, political and financial fields.'

This paragraph resulted from expediency, when the PLO was set up, to reassure the Arab states that the new organisation had no territorial ambitions. In 1968 the self-confidence of the PLO had apparently increased and this limiting article, which denied the PLO's political aspirations, was found to be superfluous.

Al-Hamma was mentioned as part of the territory of mandate Palestine, which since 1948 had been under Syrian administration. In the Arab League debates on the Palestinian entity in the years prior to the establishment of the PLO, the Syrians proposed to return al-Hamma to the Palestinian entity, since they advocated that the Palestinian organisations be an entity in control of territory; Syria demanded that Egypt and Jordan surrender the Gaza Strip and the West Bank, respectively, to this entity.

Article 26

The Palestinian Liberation Organisation, representative of the Palestinian revolutionary forces, is responsible for the Palestinian Arab people's movement in its struggle—to retrieve its homeland, liberate and return to it and exercise the right to self-determination in it—in all military, political and financial fields and also for whatever may be required by the Palestine case on the inter-Arab and international levels.

In comparison with the earlier version (Article 25), the addition here is in the stress on the fact that the PLO embodies the 'Palestinian revolutionary forces.' This addition may indicate the participation of the Fedayeen organisations in existence at the time of the 4th Council, as all these organisations claimed to be the bearers of the 'Palestinian revolution.' At this Council a change in the composition of the membership as compared with earlier councils took place. As a result of negotiations between the PLO establishment and the Fedayeen organisations, the composition of the Council was reduced from 460 (in the 3rd PNC) to 100 members of which 32 delegates were from the PLO and the Palestinian trade unions, 20 from the Palestinian Liberation Army, 38 from Fatah and the other Fedayeen organisations that conferred with it in Cairo in January 1968, and ten from the Popular Front (PFLP).

The term 'the Palestinian revolution' generally denotes the activity of the Palestinians in their struggle. In the new version, the PLO also has a role after victory—to concretise the right of self-determination.

Article 27

The Palestine Liberation Organisation shall cooperate with all Arab states, each according to its potentialities; and will adopt a neutral policy among them in the light of the requirements of the

war of liberation; and on this basis it shall not interfere in the internal affairs of any Arab state.

The phrase 'will adopt a neutral policy . . . war of liberation' is an addition to the previous text. The commitment to neutrality in inter-Arab disputes and non-interference in the internal affairs of the Arab states is not unreserved. It is made conditional on the needs of the Palestinian struggle, i.e., as long as that struggle does not require such intervention. This article therefore expresses a tougher attitude by the PLO toward the Arab states than it could afford in 1964. The validity of this article is based on Articles 14 and 15, which affirm that the struggle against Israel is bound up with the fate of all the Arab states. Thus the absolutist tenor of the PLO towards Israel spills over into its relations with the Arab states.

Shafīq al-Hūt, the head of the PLO bureau in Beirut, spelled out PLO claims to the right to such an intervention: 'The organisation [PLO] considers that it has a right and an obligation to intervene in any Arab or international situation which positively or negatively affects the Palestinian problem. The intensity of such an intervention and its magnitude will accord with the intensity and magnitude of the emergency as regards the problem' (*Facts about the Road to Liberation*, p. 18).

The PLO did not keep to its commitment to non-intervention in the internal affairs of Arab states in two prominent cases: in Jordan, up to September 1970 and in Lebanon, where intervention persisted and reached its peak in 1976. Indeed, in the debate about PLO's behaviour in Lebanon, the Syrians and the Syrian Fedayeen organisations, Sa'iqa and PLA (Palestinian Army), charged the PLO establishment with contravening this article by its intervention in Lebanon.

Article 28

The Palestinian Arab people assert the genuineness and independence of their national (wataniyya) revolution and reject all forms of intervention, trusteeship and subordination.

This is a new article, which in content is a continuation of the previous one in presenting a firm Palestinian stand. The Palestinian movement is independent, is not a pawn of any Arab state, and does not take orders from any outside authority.

It is true that the first Arab summit meeting in January 1964 did not set up the PLO. Yet, without the permission it gave Shuqairy to survey the opinions of the Palestinians on the question of how they should be organised, Shuqairy could not have taken an initiative to set up the PLO. However, the stress on 'genuineness' (authenticity) is meant to affirm that the PLO was created entirely as a result of a Palestinian effort. The claim that the PLO is Palestinian from the start is intended to support its claim to independence.

Actually the Palestinian movement arose at the beginning of the 1960s in protest and in opposition to the Arab states and pan-Arab parties (such as Ba'th, Qawmiyyun, the Nasserites etc.) whose behaviour concerning the Palestinian cause was a disappointment to the Palestinians. The Arab states were suspicious of an independent Palestinian organisation and for some years prevented its creation. The establishment of the PLO was due to inter-Arab rivalries, as the Arab states competed in manifestations of support for the establishment of a 'Palestinian entity,' even though in practice they frequently put obstacles in the Palestinians' way.

The relationship between the PLO and the Arab states was bedevilled by ambivalences, as theoretical independence and non-intervention contradicted the daily developments and their needs. The PLO has opposed the policies of all the Arab states at different times, but nevertheless is dependent on them, as without their support and hospitality the PLO is practically powerless.

It should be noted that the 7th summit conference in Rabat (29 October 1974) promulgated a resolution in which this demand for the independence of the Palestinian movement was recognised: All Arab states 'commit themselves to preserve the Palestinian national (wataniyya) unity and the non-intervention in the internal affairs of the Palestinian action.'

The demand for independence for the Palestinians has taken on a special importance after the war in Lebanon in 1977 as Arab states, such as Syria and Egypt demand that the PLO adapt to their policies. Any such demand, not to mention a positive response to it, is denounced in PLO internal debates as a violation of this article.

Article 29

The Palestinian people possess the fundamental and genuine legal right to liberate and retrieve their homeland. The Palestinian people determine their attitude toward all states and forces on the basis of the stands they adopt vis-à-vis the Palestinian case and the extent of the support they offer to the Palestinian revolution to fulfil the aims of the Palestinian people.

The first sentence would have been superfluous if it had been intended to assert the Palestinians' right as compared to the Israelis' right to Palestine which has already been as emphatically repudiated. It seems that the thrust of this article is directed toward the Arab states, i.e., that the Palestinians are the final arbiter as to the line of policy to be adopted. It thus goes further than Article 27 which dealt with the modality of cooperation with the Arab states. There is too a veiled admonishment that the PLO will retaliate against the Arab states, and even other states, if they take a line of policy which the PLO regards as inimical to its cause. Arab states have to conform to PLO wishes.

During the Khartoum summit conference (29 August–1 September 1967) Shuqairy tried to have the conference explicitly acknowledge the PLO as having the right to determine the general Arab policy in the conflict. In an interview concerning the conference he stated that other Arab states as well, such as Algeria, Tunisia, Libya and Morocco, had demanded for themselves the sole right to define their aspirations (the goals) in their struggle, relegating the other Arab states to a supporting role: 'I asked them one by one: "did you yourselves not decide once and for all on your self-determination and the struggle was then placed on your shoulders, while the role of the Arab states was to help and support you, leaving you the last word?" If so, why should the Palestinian people not have the same right in having the last word in laying down its self-determination and in deciding on the kind of political solution to the problem of Palestine whether to accept or reject. Why do you deprive us of our right?' (*Shu'un Filastiniyya*, No. 4, September 1971, p. 96).

Shuqairy's demand that was rejected by the Arab rulers in Khartoum was accepted by them in the Algiers summit conference (28 November 1973) and reconfirmed at the Rabat summit conference (29 October 1974). The resolutions of both conferences stated: 'Commitment [Arabic-*iltizam*, by Arab states, Y.H.] to the restoration of the national right of the Palestinian people will be according to the decision of the PLO in its capacity as the sole representative of the Palestinian people.' (The secret resolutions of the Algiers conference were published in the Lebanese daily *Al-Nahar* of 4 December 1973.) Thus the Arab states endorsed all future demands on the most basic issue—what is an acceptable solution to the conflict.

The threat that the PLO would formulate its stand toward any Arab state in accordance with its position on the conflict echoes a similar principle laid down at the first Arab summit concerning the attitude of the Arab states toward foreign governments.

Article 30
Fighters and carriers of arms in the war of liberation are the nucleus of the popular army which will be the protective force for the gains of the Palestinian Arab people.

This is a new article, which was decided on when the PLO became a framework for the Fedayeen organisations. In other words, there will be a continuation to the Fedayeen career or to service in the Palestinian army.

Article 31
The PLO shall have a flag, an oath of allegiance and an anthem. All this shall be decided upon in accordance with a special regulation.

This is the same as Article 27 in the previous version.

Article 32
Basic regulations of the Palestinian Liberation Organisation shall be annexed to this Charter. It shall lay down the manner in which the Organisation, and its organs and institutions shall be constituted; the respective competence of each; and the requirements of its obligations under the Charter.

This is the same as Article 28 in the previous version. Such regulations which form the Constitution of the PLO were defined at the 1st Council and amended by the 4th (see Appendix C). The main changes introduced in 1968 concerned the question of the composition of the National Council once the PLO had become a federation of Fedayeen organisations, and the method of selecting the chairman and members of the PLO's Executive Committee.

Article 33
This Charter shall not be amended save by [vote of] a majority of two-thirds of the total membership of the national congress of the Palestinian Liberation Organisation [taken] at a special session convened for that purpose.

Identical with Article 29 of the earlier version. The resolutions of the Palestinian National Councils are passed by a majority vote of those present (the legal quorum in a council is two-thirds of all members); while any amendment of the Covenant requires a larger majority reckoned not on the basis of presence but membership—i.e., two-thirds of the PNC's members.

Notes

1. Ahmed Shuqairy is a Palestinian politician (born in 1907 in Lebanon). From 1957 he served as Minister of State of Saudi Arabia and its delegate to the UN. In 1963 he was dismissed for his refusal to lodge a complaint at the UN against Egyptian intervention in Yemen. In September 1963 he was appointed by the Arab League as 'the Representative of Palestine' at League meetings. In this capacity he founded the PLO and served as its leader (officially—Chairman of its Executive Committee) until December 1967. He was succeeded in February 1969 by Yasser Arafat.
2. The Fundamental Law (*al-nizām al-asāsi*) defines the structure of PLO, its subdivisions and rules of procedure. There is no consistency in the English nomenclature of PLO institutions as used by PLO circles themselves. The same document is also referred to as 'The PLO Constitution' (see Appendix C).
3. The names of sources are given in the text in an abridged form. Full names are listed at the end.
4. The legislature of the PLO or its 'parliament' (*al-majlis al-filastini al-watani*—the 'Palestinian National Council', 'Assembly', or 'Congress' as its name is usually rendered in English) is the supreme authority of the PLO and meets irregularly, from as often as twice a year to once in three years such as the last (the 13th in March 1977). Its composition has varied over the years from 100 to 500 delegates.
5. The liquidation of Israel or the liberation of Palestine, which in practice are synonymous, are substantiated by the following considerations: a definition in principle and in essence of Palestine and the Palestinians that Palestine is inseparable from the Arab homeland (Article 1); the principle that Palestine is indivisible (Article 2); the Palestinians are the owners of Palestine (Article 3); the Palestinians have the right of self-determination and sovereignty over all of Palestine (Articles 9, 18 and 19); the liberation of Palestine will lead to Arab unity—a utilitarian argument (Article 13); the liberation of Palestine is a necessity constituting a fateful question for pan-Arabism —a historical conception (Article 14); the liberation of Palestine is an all-Arab national duty to forestall threats of aggression—a utilitarian argument (Article 15); liberation will bring tranquility and freedom of worship—utilitarian and humanistic argument (Article 16); thus alienation and subjugation of the Palestinians will end—a social and political argument (Articles 17, 18); this is an act of self-defence that will

abolish an illegal state of affairs—a legal argument; liberation will make peace and order possible—a utilitarian argument (Article 18); the elimination of the existence of Israel springs from the will of the Palestinians—an arbitrary definition; and from their natural right to their homeland and self-determination in accordance with United Nations principles—a philosophical and legal definition (Article 19); the right to a Jewish National Home is a travesty of international legality and decency, the historical rights of the Jews are spurious, the Jews are not a nation—historical and intrinsic arguments (Article 20); the existence of Israel prevents the full liberation of Palestine— political argument (Article 21); Israel is the incarnation of Zionism, a negative phenomenon that threatens the whole world, whose elimin- ation is required for world order—intrinsic, political and utilitarian arguments (Article 22).

6. I do not pretend at all that Zionism or Israel are impeccable. For years I viewed with many misgivings the possibility that the greater the Arab threat to Israel the greater the liberty or license Israel might take to defend itself in a fashion that deviates from moral norms. In a conflict in which one side takes an absolutist position there may be a tendency for the other side also to revert to absolutist ideas. This book is only a practical account of the conflict as it deals with one side. My basic criticism of Zionism and Israel is propounded in a long essay, *Israel's position in the Arab-Israeli Conflict*, in Hebrew, Dvir, Tel-Aviv, 1968. A partial French translation was included in *Les Temps Modernes* No. 253 bis, 1967. I ask the reader not to attribute to me what he or she thinks are the policy conclusions following from my analysis of the Covenant. My evaluation of both Arab and Israeli positions at the present stage with my policy prescription for Israel is the subject of my recent book *Arab Strategies and Israel's Response*, NY, The Free Press, 1977.

7. The Rejection Front is a group of Fedayeen organisations, among which the PFLP predominates, opposing any attempt at a political solution, who stress that violence is the only way to attain their objectives. They reject PLO participation in a Geneva conference.

8. An intermediary body above the Executive Committee but below a PNC which was created by the 7th PNC to 'decide on urgent and emergency matters in a manner consistent with the provisions of the Palestinian National Covenant' (*International Documents on Palestine, 1970*, p. 827). It subsequently fell into abeyance but was reactivated by the 11th PNC. It comprises at the present stage 55 members and meets irregularly. The PFLP does not participate in it.

9. The translation of the Covenant follows the English version in Leila S. Kadi, *Basic Documents of the Armed Palestinian Resistance Movement*, PLO Research Centre, Beirut, 1969, pp. 137–42.

   Another English translation is found in Zuhair Diab (ed), *International Documents on Palestine, 1968*, The Institute for Palestine Studies, Beirut, 1971, pp. 393–5. The differences between these two translations are not significant. I preferred the first translation, since it seems to be the one mostly used in PLO publications, though the second is better from the point of view of language (see Appendix B2).

10. Significantly, the Palestine Royal Commission (under the chairmanship of Earl Peel), appointed to investigate the situation in Palestine, referred in their report (July 1937) to the Arabs in Palestine only as 'Arabs'. It summarised their claims and political configuration under the heading of Arab Nationalism, not Palestinian Nationalism (p. 130).

11. These differentiations are new. *Wataniyya* is an old expression and a positive quality connected with a saying attributed to the Prophet—'Love of one's *watan* [originally the place where one lived] follows from faith'. *Qawmiyya* is a new coinage.

Bibliography

Ibrahim al-'Abid, *Guide to the Palestine Problem, Questions and Answers,* (Arabic) PLO Research Center, Beirut, 1969.

Ibrahim al-'Abid, *A Handbook to the Palestinian Question, Questions and Answers,* PLO Research Center, 1971.

Nāji 'Alūsh, *The Road to Palestine* (Arabic), Moanshūrāt Dār al-Tali'a, Beirut, 1964.

Nāji 'Alūsh, *The Palestinian National Movement Vis-à-vis the Jews and Zionism 1882–1948,* (Arabic), Dār al-Nahār, Beirut, 1969.

Dr. Mundhir Fāiq 'Anabtāwi, *Documents of Palestine 1965* (Arabic), The Institute for Palestine Studies, Beirut, 1966.

Burhān al-Dajāni (ed.) *The Palestine Yearbook 1968* (Arabic), The Institute for Palestine Studies, Beirut, 1971.

Burhān al-Dajāni, (ed.) *The Palestine Yearbook, 1965,* (Arabic), The Institute for Palestine Studies, Beirut, 1967.

Zuhair Diāb (ed.) *International Documents on Palestine, 1968,* The Institute for Palestine Studies, Beirut, 1971.

Dirāsāt 'Arabiyya (Arab Studies), A monthly Cultural and Social Review, Dār al-Tali'a, Beirut.

Niqula al-Dur, *Thus Lost and thus Returned, the Role of Oil and the Gun in the Liberation of Palestine,* (Arabic), Dār al-Hawādith Press, Beirut, 1963.

Fatah, *Liberation of the Occupied Lands and the Method of Struggle Against Direct Colonialism,* Revolutionary Studies and experiences, No. 8, Sept. 1967, No place of publication given.

Fatah, Office of Public Relations and Indoctrination, *The Relationship Between the Palestine Revolution and the Arab and World Revolutions,* (Arabic), Dār al-Djihād Press, Cairo, no date, 38 pages.

Fatah, Central Public Relations, *Fatah Yearbook 1968,* Distribution by Dār al-Tali'a, Beirut, no date, 480 pages.

Fateh, (English) March 23, 1971, POB 5427, Beirut, Lebanon.

Y. Harkabi, "Vautours et colombes" in *Le Conflict israëlo-arabe,* Les Temps Modernes No. 253 bis, 1967, pp. 472-501.

Y. Harkabi, *Fedayeen Action and Arab Strategy,* Adelphi Paper 53, The International Institute for Strategic Studies, London, December 1968.

Y. Harkabi, *Arab Attitudes to Israel,* Israel University Press, or Keter Publishing House, Jerusalem 1972 and 1976.

Y. Harkabi, *Palestinians and Israel,* Keter Publishing House, Jerusalem, 1974.

Y. Harkabi, *Arab Strategies and Israel's Response,* The Free Press, New York, 1977.

Sati 'al-Husri, *Arabism First* (Arabic), Dār al-'ilm lib-mallayin, Beirut, 4th print, 1961.

Shafiq al Hūt, *Facts about the Road to Liberation,* PLO Research Center, Beirut, 1966.

Journal of Palestine Studies, Editor Hisham Sharabi, The Institute for Palestine Studies and Kuwait University.

Leila S. Kādi, *Basic Political Documents of the Armed Palestinian Resistance Movement,* Palestine Books No. 27, PLO Research Center, Beirut, December, 1969.

Walid Khaddūri (Ed.) *International Documents on Palestine 1970,* The Institute for Palestine Studies, Beirut, 1973.

Walid al-Khālidī, Yusuf Anis, *Arab Documents 1964* (Arabic), The American University of Beirut.

Al-Nahār, Newspaper, Beirut.

PLO, *Al-Mājlis al-Watanī al-Filastini al-Dawra al-Thānia,* 2nd PNC, Official Report, Gaza, no date.

PLO, *The Popular Congress and Palestinian National Council, The Tenth Extraordinary Session from 6–12 April 1972* (Arabic Official Report) no date, no place, 192 pages.

Palestine Lives, Interviews with Leaders of the Resistance, Introduction by Clovis Maksoud, Palestine Research Center and Kuwaiti Teachers' Association, 1973.

Dr. Fayez Sayegh, *A Handful of Mist—A Study of the Meaning of Bourgibism and its Slogans,* (Arabic) PLO Research Center, Beirut, 1966.

Anis Sayegh (Ed.) *Filastiniyat* (Arabic—Palestine Affairs) PLO Research Center, Beirut, 1968.

Seminar of Arab Jurists on Palestine, Algiers 22–27 July 1967, *The Palestine Question,* Translated from French by Edward Rizk, The Institute for Palestine Studies, Beirut, 1968.

Ahmed Shuqairy, *Forty Years in Arab and International Life,* (Arabic) Dar al-Nahar, Beirut, 1969.

Ahmed Shuqairy, *From the Summit to Defeat, with the Kings and Presidents* (Arabic) Dar al-'Auda, Beirut, 1971.

Shu'ūn Filastiniyya, (Palestine Affairs) a periodical published by PLO Research Center in Beirut.

V. Vance et P. Laner, *Hussein de Jordanie: ma guerre avec Israël,* Paris, Albin Michel, 1968.

Anne Zahlān, *International Documents on Palestine 1971,* Institute for Palestine Studies, Beirut, 1974.

APPENDICES

A. *The Palestinian National Covenant, 1964*
    Sadat Hasan, *Introducing the Palestine Liberation Organiza-tion*, PLO, 801 2nd Ave. N.Y. 10017, pp. 12–14.

B. *The Palestinian National Covenant, 1968*
    1) The English translation as in Leila S. Kadi, *Basic Political Documents of the Armed Resistance Movement*, PLO, Research Center, Beirut, 1969, pp. 137–142.
    2) The English translation as in Zuhair Diab (ed.) *International Documents on Palestine, 1968*, The Institute for Palestine Studies, Beirut, 1971, pp. 393–5.

C. *The Constitution of the Palestine Liberation Organization* (*Ibid.*, pp. 396–398).

D. *The Political Program of the PLO* (January 1973, promul-gated by the 11th PNC) *Palestine Lives*, Palestine Research Center and the Kuwaiti Teachers' Association, Beirut, 1973, pp. 157–67.

E. *Political Programme for the Present Stage Drawn up by the 12th PNC* (June 9, 1974) from *The Journal of Palestine Studies* Vol. 3, No. 4, Summer 1974, p. 224.

F. *Political Resolutions of the 13th PNC* (March 20, 1977) with commentaries by Y. Harkabi, *Jerusalem Post*, March 29, 1977 (revised version).

Appendix A

IN THE NAME OF THE ALMIGHTY, THE MAGNIFICENT
THE MOST MERCIFUL
THE PALESTINIAN NATIONAL COVENANT

INTRODUCTION

We. The Palestinian Arab people, who waged fierce and continuous battles to safeguard its homeland, to defend its dignity and honour, and who offered, all through the years, continuous caravans of immortal martyrs, and who wrote the noblest pages of sacrifice, offering and giving.

We, the Palestinian Arab people, who faced the forces of evil, injustice and aggression, against whom the forces of International Zionism and colonialism conspired and worked to displace it, dispossess it from its homeland and property, abused what is holy in it and who in spite of all this refused to weaken or submit.

We. The Palestinian Arab people, who believe in its Arabism and in its right to regain its homeland to realize its freedom and dignity and who has determined to amass its forces and mobilize its efforts and capabilities in order to continue its struggle and to move forward on the path of holy war until complete and final victory has been attained.

We. The Palestinian Arab people, depending upon our right of self-defense and the complete restoration of our lost homeland — a right that has been recognized by international covenants and common practices including the charter of the United Nations and in implementation of the principles of human rights' and comprehending the international political relations, with its various ramifications and limits, and considering the past experiences in all that pertains to the causes of the catastrophe, and the means to face it.

And embarking from the Palestine Arab reality, and for the sake of the honour of the Palestinian individual and his right to free and dignified life;

And realizing the national grave responsibility placed upon our shoulders, for the sake of all this.

We, the Palestinian Arab people, dictate and declare this Palestinian National Covenant and vow to realize it.

Article 1. Palestine is an Arab homeland bound by strong national ties to the rest of the Arab Countries and which together form the large Arab homeland.

Article 2. Palestine with its boundaries at the time of the British Mandate is a regional indivisible unit.

Article 3. The Palestinian Arab people has the legitimate right to its homeland and is an inseparable part of the Arab Nation. It shares the sufferings and aspirations of the Arab Nation and its struggle for freedom, sovereignty, progress and unity.

Article 4. The people of Palestine determines its destiny when it completes the liberation of its homeland in accordance with its own wishes and free will and choice.

Article 5. The Palestinian personality is a permanent and genuine charactaristic that does not disappear. It is transferred from fathers to sons.

Article 6. The Palestinians are those Arab citizens who were living normally in Palestine up to 1947, whether they remained or were expelled. Every child who was born to a Palestinian parent after this date whether in Palestine or outside is a Palestinian.

Article 7. Jews of Palestinian origin are considered Palestinians if they are willing to live peacefully and loyally in Palestine.

Article 8. Bringing up Palestinian youth in Arab and nationalist manner is a fundamental national duty. All means of guidance education and enlightenment should be utilized to introduce the youth to its homeland in a deep spiritual way that will constantly and firmly bind them together.

Article 9. Doctrines whether political social or economic, shall not occupy the people of Palestine from the primary duty of liberating their homeland. All Palestinians constitute one national front and work with all their feelings and spiritual and material potentialities to free their homeland.

Article 10. Palestinians have three mottos: National unity, National mobilization; and Liberation. Once liberation is completed, the people of Palestine shall choose for its public life whatever political economic or social system they want.

Article 11. The Palestinian people firmly believe in Arab unity, and in order to play its role in realizing this goal, it must, at this stage of its struggle preserve its Palestinian personality and all its constituents. It must strengthen the consciousness of its existence and stand against any attempt or plan that may weaken or disintegrate its personality.

Article 12. Arab unity and the liberation of Palestine are two complementary goals; each prepares for the attainment of the other. Arab unity leads to the liberation of Palestine, and the liberation of Palestine leads to Arab unity. Working for both must go side by side.

Article 13. The destiny of the Arab Nation and even the essence of Arab existence are firmly tied to the destiny of the Palestine question; from this firm bond stems the effort and struggle of the Arab Nation to liberate Palestine. The People of Palestine assumes a vanguard role in achieving this sacred national goal.

Article 14. The liberation of Palestine from an Arab view point, is a national duty. Its responsibilities fall upon the entire Arab Nation, Governments and peoples, the Palestinian people being in the foreground. For this purpose the Arab Nation must mobilize its military spiritual and material potentialities, specifically, it must give to the Palestinian Arab people all possible support and backing and place at its disposal all opportunities and means to enable them to perform their roles in liberating their homeland.

Article 15. The liberation of Palestine, from a spiritual view point, prepares for the Holy Land, an atmosphere of tranquility and peace, in which all the Holy places will be safeguarded, and the free worship and visit to all will be guaranteed, without any discrimination of race, colour, tongue, or religion. For all this, the Palestinian people look forward to the support of all the spiritual forces in the world.

Article 16. The liberation of Palestine from an international view point is a defensive act necessitated by the demands of self defense as stated in the charter of the United Nations. That is why the people of Palestine desiring to befriend all nations which love freedom, justice, and peace, is looking forward for their support in restoring the legitimate situation to Palestine, establishing peace and security in its territory, and enable its people to exercise national sovereignty and freedom.

Article 17. The Partitioning of Palestine in 1947 and the establishment of Israel are illegal and false regardless of the loss of time, because they were contrary to the wish of the Palestine people and its natural right to its homeland, and in violation of the basic principles embodied in the charter of the United Nations, foremost among which is the right to self-determination.

Article 18. The Balfour Declaration, the Mandate system and all that has been based upon them are considered fraud. The claims of historic and spiritual ties, ties between Jews and Palestine are not in agreement with the facts of history or with the true basis of sound statehood. Judaism because it is a divine religion is not a nationality with independent existence. Furthermore the Jews are not one people with an independent personality because they are citizens of the countries to which they belong.

Article 19. Zionism is a colonialist movement in its inception, aggressive and expansionist in its goals, racist and segregationist in its configurations and fascist in its means and aims. Israel in its capacity as the spearhead of this destructive movement and the pillar for colonialism is a permanent source of tension and turmoil in the Middle East in particular and to the international community in general. Because of this the people of Palestine are worthy of the support and sustenance of the community of nations.

Article 20. The causes of peace and security and the needs of right and justice demand from all nations, in order to safeguard true relationships among peoples, and to maintain the loyalty of citizens to their homeland, to consider Zionism an illegal movement and to outlaw its presence and activities.

Article 21. The Palestine people believes in the principle of justice, freedom, sovereignty, self determination, human dignity, and the right of peoples to practice these principles. It also supports all international efforts to bring about peace on the basis of justice and free international co-operation.

Article 22. The people of Palestine believe in peaceful coexistence on the basis of legal existence, for there can be no coexistence with aggression, nor can there be peace with occupation and colonialism.

Article 23. In realizing the goals and principles of this Covenant the Palestine Liberation Organization carries out its complete role to liberate Palestine in accordance with the fundamental Law of this Organization.

Article 24. This Organization does not exercise any regional sovereignty over the Western Bank in the Hashimite Kingdom of Jordan, on the Gaza Strip or the Himmah Area. Its activities will be on the national popular level in the liberational, organizational, political and financial fields.

Article 25. This Organization is encharged with the movement of the Palestine people in its struggle to liberate its homeland in all liberational, organizational, political, and financial matters, and in all other needs of the Palestine Question in the Arab and international spheres.

Article 26. The Liberation Organization co-operates with all Arab governments each according to its ability, and does not interfere in the internal affairs of any Arab State.

Article 27. This Organization shall have its flag, oath and a national anthem. All this shall be resolved in accordance with a special system.

Article 28. The Fundamental Law for the Palestine Liberation Organization is attached to this Covenant. This

Law defines the manner of establishing the Organization, its organs, institutions, the specialties of each one of them, and all the needed duties thrust upon it in accordance with this Covenant.

Article 29. This Covenant cannot be amended except by two-thirds majority of the National Council of the Palestine Liberation Organization in a special session called for this purpose.

Appendix B1

THE PALESTINIAN NATIONAL CHARTER

(Palestine Liberation Organization)*

Article 1. Palestine is the homeland of the Arab Palestinian people; it is an indivisible part of the Arab homeland, and the Palestinian people are an integral part of the Arab nation.

Article 2. Palestine, with the boundaries it had during the British mandate, is an indivisible territorial unit.

Article 3. The Palestinian Arab people possess the legal right to their homeland and have the right to determine their destiny after achieving the liberation of their country in accordance with their wishes and entirely of their own accord and will.

Article 4. The Palestinian identity is a genuine, essential and inherent characteristic; it is transmitted from parents to children. The Zionist occupation and the dispersal of the Palestinian Arab people, through the disasters which befell them, do not make them lose their Palestinian identity and their membership of the Palestinian community, nor do they negate them.

Article 5. The Palestinians are those Arab nationals who, until 1947, normally resided in Palestine regardless of whether they were evicted from it or have stayed there. Anyone born, after that date, of a Palestinian father—whether inside Palestine or outside it—is also a Palestinian.

Article 6. The Jews who had normally resided in Palestine until the beginning of the Zionist invasion will be considered Palestinians.

(*) Decisions of the National Congress of the Palestine Liberation Organization held in Cairo from 1–17 July 1968.

Article 7. That there is a Palestinian community and that it has material, spiritual and historical connection with Palestine are indisputable facts. It is a national duty to bring up individual Palestinians in an Arab revolutionary manner. All means of information and education must be adopted in order to acquaint the Palestinian with his country in the most profound manner, both spiritual and material, that is possible. He must be prepared for the armed struggle and ready to sacrifice his wealth and his life in order to win back his homeland and bring about its liberation.

Article 8. The phase in their history, through which the Palestinian people are now living, is that of national struggle for the liberation of Palestine. Thus the conflicts among the Palestinian national forces are secondary, and should be ended for the sake of the basic conflict that exists between the forces of Zionism and of imperialism on the one hand. and the Palestinian Arab people on the other. On this basis the Palestinian masses, regardless of whether they are residing in the national homeland or in diaspora, constitute—both their organizations and the individuals—one national front working for the retrieval of Palestine and its liberation through armed struggle.

Article 9. Armed struggle is the only way to liberate Palestine. Thus it is the overall strategy, not merely a tactical phase. The Palestinian Arab people assert their absolute determination and firm resolution to continue their armed struggle and to work for an armed popular revolution for the liberation of their country and their return to it. They also assert their right to normal life in Palestine and to exercise their right to self-determination and sovereignty over it.

Article 10. Commando action constitutes the nucleus of the Palestinian popular liberation war. This requires its escalation, comprehensiveness and the mobilization of all the Palestinian popular and educational efforts and their organization and involvement in the armed Palestinian revolution. It also requires the achieving of unity for the national struggle among the different groupings of the Palestinian people, and between the Palestinian people and the Arab masses so as to secure the continuation of the revolution, its escalation and victory.

Article 11. The Palestinians will have three mottoes: national unity, national mobilization and liberation.

Article 12. The Palestinian people believe in Arab unity. In order to contribute their share towards the attainment of that objective, however, they must, at the present stage of their struggle, safeguard their Palestinian identity and develop their consciousness of that identity, and oppose any plan that may dissolve or impair it.

Article 13. Arab unity and the liberation of Palestine are two complementary objectives, the attainment of either of which facilitates the attainment of the other. Thus, Arab unity leads to the liberation of Palestine; the liberation of Palestine leads to Arab unity; and work towards the realization of one objective proceeds side by side with work towards the realization of the other.

Article 14. The destiny of the Arab nation, and indeed Arab existence itself, depends upon the destiny of the Palestine cause. From this interdependence springs the Arab nation's pursuit of, and striving for, the liberation of Palestine. The people of Palestine play the role of the vanguard in the realization of this sacred national goal.

Article 15. The liberation of Palestine, from an Arab viewpoint, is a national duty and it attempts to repel the Zionist and imperialist aggression against the Arab homeland, and aims at the elimination of Zionism in Palestine. Absolute responsibility for this falls upon the Arab nation—peoples and governments—with the Arab people of Palestine in the vanguard. Accordingly the Arab nation must mobilize all its military, human, moral and spiritual capabilities to participate actively with the Palestinian people in the liberation of Palestine. It must, particularly in the phase of the armed Palestinian revolution, offer and furnish the Palestinian people with all possible help, and material and human support, and make available to them the means and opportunities that will enable them to continue to carry out their leading role in the armed revolution, until they liberate their homeland.

Article 16. The liberation of Palestine, from a spiritual point of view, will provide the Holy Land with an atmosphere of safety and tranquillity, which in turn will safeguard the country's religious sanctuaries and guarantee freedom of worship and of visit to all, without discrimination of race, color, language, or religion. Accordingly, the people of Palestine look to all spiritual forces in the world for support.

Article 17. The liberation of Palestine, from a human point of view, will restore to the Palestinian individual his dignity, pride and freedom. Accordingly the Palestinian Arab people look forward to the support of all those who believe in the dignity of man and his freedom in the world.

Article 18. The liberation of Palestine, from an international point of view, is a defensive action necessitated by the demands of self-defence. Accordingly, the Palestinian people, desirous as they are of the friendship of all people, look to freedom-loving, justice-loving and peace-loving states for support in order to restore their legitimate rights in Palestine, to re-establish peace and security in the country, and to enable its people to exercise national sovereignty and freedom.

Article 19. The partition of Palestine in 1947 and the establishment of the state of Israel are entirely illegal, regardless of the passage of time, because they were contrary to the will of the Palestinian people and to their natural right in their homeland, and inconsistent with the principles embodied in the Charter of the United Nations, particularly the right to self-determination.

Article 20. The Balfour Declaration, the mandate for Palestine and everything that has been based upon them, are deemed null and void. Claims of historical or religious ties of Jews with Palestine are incompatible with the facts of history and the true conception of what constitutes statehood. Judaism, being a religion, is not an independent nationality. Nor do Jews constitute a single nation with an identity of its own; they are citizens of the states to which they belong.

Article 21. The Arab Palestinian people, expressing themselves by the armed Palestinian revolution, reject all solutions which are substitutes for the total liberation of Palestine and reject all proposals aiming at the liquidation of the Palestinian problem, or its internationalization.

Article 22. Zionism is a political movement organically associated with international imperialism and antagonistic to all action for liberation and to progressive movements in the world. It is racist and fanatic in its nature, aggressive, expansionist and colonial in its aim, and fascist in its methods. Israel is the instrument of the Zionist movement, and a geographical base for world imperialism placed strategically in the midst of the Arab homeland to combat the hopes of the Arab nation for liberation, unity and progress. Israel is a constant source of threat *vis-à-vis* peace in the Middle East and the whole world. Since the liberation of Palestine will destroy the Zionist and imperialist presence and will contribute to the establishment of peace in the Middle East, the Palestinian people look for the support of all the progressive and peaceful forces and urge them all, irrespective of their affiliations and beliefs, to offer the Palestinian people all aid and support in their just struggle for the liberation of their homeland.

Article 23. The demands of security and peace, as well as the demands of right and justice, require all states to consider Zionism an illegitimate movement, to outlaw its existence, and to ban its operations, in order that friendly relations among peoples may be preserved, and the loyalty of citizens to their respective homelands safeguarded.

Article 24. The Palestinian people believe in the principles of justice, freedom, sovereignty, self-determination, human dignity, and in the right of all peoples to exercise them.

Article 25. For the realization of the goals of this Charter and its principles, the Palestine Liberation Organization will perform its role in the liberation of Palestine in accordance with the Constitution of this Organization.

Article 26. The Palestine Liberation Organization, representative of the Palestinian revolutionary forces, is responsible for the Palestinian Arab people's movement in its struggle—to retrieve its homeland, liberate and return to it and exercise the right to self-determination in it—in all military, political and financial fields and also for whatever may be required by the Palestine case on the inter-Arab and international levels.

Article 27. The Palestine Liberation Organization shall cooperate with all Arab states, each according to its potentialities; and will adopt a neutral policy among them in the light of the requirements of the war of liberation; and on this basis it shall not interfere in the internal affairs of any Arab state.

Article 28. The Palestinian Arab people assert the genuineness and independence of their national revolution and reject all forms of intervention, trusteeship and subordination.

Article 29. The Palestinian people possess the fundamental and genuine legal right to liberate and retrieve their homeland. The Palestinian people determine their attitude towards all states and forces on the basis of the stands they adopt *vis-à-vis* the Palestinian case and the extent of the support they offer to the Palestinian revolution to fulfil the aims of the Palestinian people.

Article 30. Fighters and carriers of arms in the war of liberation are the nucleus of the popular army which will be the protective force for the gains of the Palestinian Arab people.

Article 31. The Organization shall have a flag, an oath of allegiance and an anthem. All this shall be decided upon in accordance with a special regulation.

Article 32. Regulations, which shall be known as the Constitution of the Palestine Liberation Organization, shall be annexed to this Charter. It shall lay down the manner in which the Organization, and its organs and institutions, shall be constituted; the respective competence of each; and the requirements of its obligations under the Charter.

Article 33. This Charter shall not be amended save by (vote of) a majority of two-thirds of the total membership of the National Congress of the Palestine Liberation Organization (taken) at a special session convened for that purpose.

Appendix B2

The Palestine National Charter Adopted by the Fourth Palestine National Assembly.[1]

Cairo, July 17, 1968

1. This Charter shall be known as "the Palestine National Charter."

Articles of the Charter:

Article 1. Palestine, the homeland of the Palestinian Arab people, is an inseparable part of the greater Arab homeland, and the Palestinian people are a part of the Arab Nation.

Article 2. Palestine, within the frontiers that existed under the British Mandate, is an indivisible territorial unit.

Article 3. The Palestinian Arab people alone have legitimate rights to their homeland, and shall exercise the right of self-determination after the liberation of their homeland, in keeping with their wishes and entirely of their own accord.

Article 4. The Palestinian identity is an authentic, intrinsic and indissoluble quality that is transmitted from father to son. Neither the Zionist occupation nor the dispersal of the Palestinian Arab people as a result of the afflictions they have suffered can efface this Palestinian identity.

Article 5. Palestinians are Arab citizens who were normally resident in Palestine until 1947. This includes both those who were forced to leave or who stayed in Palestine. Anyone

1. Archives of the Institute for Palestine Studies. The Fourth Palestine National Assembly, held in Cairo from July 10 to 17, formed a committee to revise the Palestine National Charter adopted by the First Palestine National Conference in Jerusalem in 1964. The committee completed its task on July 15.

119

born to a Palestinian father after that date, whether inside or outside Palestine, is a Palestinian.

Article 6. Jews who were normally resident in Palestine up to the beginning of the Zionist invasion are Palestinians.

Article 7. Palestinian identity, and material, spiritual and historical links with Palestine are immutable realities. It is a national obligation to provide every Palestinian with a revolutionary Arab upbringing, and to instil in him a profound spiritual and material familiarity with his homeland and a readiness for armed struggle and for the sacrifice of his material possessions and his life, for the recovery of his homeland. All available educational means and means of guidance must be enlisted to that end, until liberation is achieved.

Article 8. The Palestinian people is at the stage of national struggle for the liberation of its homeland. For that reason, differences between Palestinian national forces must give way to the fundamental difference that exists between Zionism and imperialism on the one hand and the Palestinian Arab people on the other. On that basis, the Palestinian masses, both as organizations and as individuals, whether in the homeland or in such places as they now live as refugees, constitute a single national front working for the recovery and liberation of Palestine through armed struggle.

Article 9. Armed struggle is the only way of liberating Palestine, and is thus strategic, not tactical. The Palestinian Arab people hereby affirm their unwavering determination to carry on the armed struggle and to press on towards popular revolution for the liberation of and return to their homeland. They also affirm their right to a normal life in their homeland, to the exercise of their right of self-determination therein and to sovereignty over it.

Article 10. Commando action constitutes the nucleus of the Palestinian popular war of liberation. This requires that commando action should be escalated, expanded and protected and that all the resources of the Palestinian masses and all scientific potentials available to them should be mobilised and organised to play their part in the armed Palestinian revolution. It also requires solidarity in national struggle among the different groups within the Palestinian people and between that people and the Arab masses, to ensure the continuity of the escalation and victory of the revolution.

Article 11. Palestinians shall have three slogans: national unity, national mobilisation and liberation.

Article 12. The Palestinian Arab people believe in Arab unity. To fulfil their role in the achievement of that objective, they must, at the present stage in their national struggle, retain their Palestinian identity and all that it involves, work for increased awareness of it and oppose all measures liable to weaken or dissolve it.

Article 13. Arab unity and the liberation of Palestine are complementary objectives; each leads to the achievement of the other. Arab unity will lead to the liberation of Palestine, and the liberation of Palestine will lead to Arab unity. To work for one is to work for both.

Article 14. The destiny of the Arab nation, indeed the continued existence of the Arabs, depends on the fate of the Palestinian cause. This interrelationship is the point of departure of the Arab endeavour to liberate Palestine. The Palestinian people are the vanguard of the movement to achieve this sacred national objective.

Article 15. The liberation of Palestine is a national obligation for the Arabs. It is their duty to repel the Zionist and imperialist invasion of the greater Arab homeland and to liquidate the Zionist presence in Palestine. The full responsibility for this belongs to the peoples and governments of the Arab nation and to the Palestinian people first and foremost.

For this reason, the task of the Arab nation is to enlist all the military, human, moral and material resources at its command to play an effective part, along with the Palestinian people, in the liberation of Palestine. Moreover, it is the task of the Arab nation, particularly at the present stage of the Palestinian armed revolution, to offer the Palestinian people all possible aid, material and manpower support, and to place at their disposal all the means and opportunities that will enable them to continue to perform their role as the vanguard of their armed revolution until the liberation of their homeland is achieved.

Article 16. On the spiritual plane, the liberation of Palestine will establish in the Holy Land an atmosphere of peace and tranquility in which all religious institutions will be safeguarded and freedom of worship and the right of visit guaranteed to all without discrimination or distinction of race, colour, language or creed. For this reason, the people of Palestine look to all spiritual forces in the world for support.

Article 17. On the human plane, the liberation of Palestine will restore to the Palestinians their dignity, integrity and freedom. For this reason, the Palestinian Arab people look to all those who believe in the dignity and freedom of man for support.

Article 18. On the international plane, the liberation of Palestine is a defensive measure dictated by the requirements of self-defence. This is why the Palestinian people, who seek to win the friendship of all peoples, look for the support of all freedom, justice and peace-loving countries in restoring the legitimate state of affairs in Palestine, establishing security and peace in it and enabling its people to exercise national sovereignty and freedom.

Article 19. The partition of Palestine, which took place in 1947, and the establishment of Israel, are fundamentally invalid, however long they last, for they contravene the will of the people of Palestine and their natural right to their homeland and contradict the principles of the United Nations Charter, foremost among which is the right of self-determination.

Article 20. The Balfour Declaration, the Mandate Instrument, and all their consequences. are hereby declared null and void. The claim of historical or spiritual links between the Jews and Palestine is neither in conformity with historical fact nor does it satisfy the requirements for statehood. Judaism is a revealed religion; it is not a separate nationality, nor are the Jews a single people with a separate identity; they are citizens of their respective countries.

Article 21. The Palestinian Arab people, expressing themselves through the Palestinian armed revolution, reject all alternatives to the total liberation of Palestine. They also reject all proposals for the liquidation or internationalisation of the Palestine problem.

Article 22. Zionism is a political movement that is organically linked with world imperialism and is opposed to all liberation movements or movements for progress in the world. The Zionist movement is essentially fanatical and racialist; its objectives involve aggression, expansion and the establishment of colonial settlements, and its methods are those of the Fascists and the Nazis. Israel acts as cat's paw for the Zionist movement, a geographic and manpower base for world imperialism and a springboard for its thrust into the Arab homeland to frustrate the aspirations of the Arab nation to liberation, unity and progress. Israel is a constant threat to peace in the Middle East and the whole world. Inasmuch as the liberation of Palestine will eliminate the Zionist and imperialist presence in that country and bring peace to the Middle East, the Palestinian people look for support to all liberals and to all forces of good, peace and progress in the world, and call on them, whatever their political convictions, for all possible aid and support in their just and legitimate struggle to liberate their homeland.

Article 23. The demands of peace and security and the exigencies of right and justice require that all nations should regard Zionism as an illegal movement and outlaw it and its activities, out of consideration for the ties of friendship between peoples and for the loyalty of citizens to their homelands.

Article 24. The Palestinian Arab people believe in justice, freedom, sovereignty, self-determination, human dignity and the right of peoples to enjoy them.

Article 25. In pursuance of the objectives set out in this charter, the Palestine Liberation Organisation shall perform its proper role in the liberation of Palestine to the full.

Article 26. The Palestine Liberation Organisation, as the representative of the forces of the Palestinian revolution, is responsible for the struggle of the Palestinian Arab people to regain, liberate and return to their homeland and to exercise the right of self-determination in that homeland, in the military, political and financial fields, and for all else that the Palestinian cause may demand, both at Arab and international levels.

Article 27. The Palestine Liberation Organisation shall cooperate with all Arab countries, each according to its means, maintaining a neutral attitude vis-à-vis these countries in accordance with the requirements of the battle of liberation, and on the basis of that factor. The Organisation shall not interfere in the internal affairs of any Arab country.

Article 28. The Palestinian Arab people hereby affirm the authenticity and independence of their national revolution and reject all forms of interference, tutelage or dependency.

Article 29. The Palestinian Arab people have the legitimate and prior right to liberate and recover their homeland, and shall define their attitude to all countries and forces in accordance with the attitude adopted by such countries and forces to the cause of the Palestinian people and with the extent of their support for that people in their revolution to achieve their objectives.

Article 30. Those who fight or bear arms in the battle of liberation form the nucleus of the popular army which will shield the achievements of the Palestinian Arab people.

Article 31. The Organisation shall have a flag, an oath of allegiance and an anthem, to be decided in accordance with appropriate regulations.

Article 32. Regulations, to be known as Basic Regulations for the Palestine Liberation Organisation, shall be appended to this Charter. These regulations shall define the structure of the Organisation, its bodies and institutions, and the powers, duties and obligations of each of them, in accordance with this Charter.

Article 33. This Charter may only be amended with a majority of two thirds of the total number of members of the National Assembly of the Palestine Liberation Organisation at a special meeting called for that purpose.

Appendix C

Constitution of the Palestine Liberation Organisation.[1]

Cairo, July 17, 1968

CHAPTER I

General Principles

Article 1. The Palestinians, in accordance with the provisions of this Constitution, form themselves into an organisation to be known as the Palestine Liberation Organisation.

Article 2. The Palestine Liberation Organisation shall exercise its responsibilities in accordance with the principles of the National Charter, the provisions of this Constitution, and such rules, provisions and resolutions as may be issued in conformity with these principles and provisions.

Article 3. Relationships within the Organisation shall be based on commitment to struggle and to national action, the different levels of the Organisation, from its base up to its collective leadership, being closely linked together on a basis of the following principles: the minority shall defer to the will of the majority, confidence of the people shall be won through persuasion, the movement of Palestinian struggle shall be continued, the armed Palestinian revolution shall be supported, and every possible effort shall be made to ensure that it continues and escalates, so that the impetus of the masses towards liberation may take its course until victory is achieved.

In implementation of this principle, the Executive Committee shall draft constitutions for the Organisation's subsidiary bodies, due regard being paid to the circumstances of

1. Archives of the Institute for Palestine Studies.
    The Fourth Palestine National Assembly, held in Cairo from 10 to 17 July, studied the constitution for the Palestine Liberation Organization and the regulations related to its structure, and introduced certain amendments.

Palestinians in all places where they are concentrated, to the circumstances of the Palestinian revolution, and to the realisation of the objectives of the Charter and the Constitution.

Article 4. All Palestinians are natural members of the Palestine Liberation Organisation, performing their duty to liberate their country in accordance with their abilities and qualifications. The Palestinian people is the base of this Organisation.

CHAPTER II

The National Assembly

Article 5. The members of the National Assembly shall be elected by the Palestinian people by direct ballot, in accordance with a system to be devised for this purpose by the Executive Committee.

Article 6. (a) Should it be impossible to hold an election to the Assembly, the National Assembly shall continue to sit until circumstances permit of the holding of elections.

(b) If, for some reason, one or more seats in the National Assembly fall vacant, the Assembly shall appoint a member or members to fill the vacant seats.

Article 7. (a) The National Assembly is the supreme authority of the Liberation Organisation. It drafts the policy, planning and programmes of the Organisation.

(b) Jerusalem is the seat of the Palestine Liberation Organisation.

Article 8. The National Assembly is elected for three years, and it shall be convened in regular session once every six months by its President or, should extraordinary sessions be necessary, by the President at the request of the Executive Committee, or of a quarter of its members. It shall meet in Jerusalem, Gaza, or any other place, depending on circumstances. Should the President not call such a session, the session shall convene automatically in such place and at such time as are designated in the request submitted by its members or by the Executive Committee.

Article 9. The National Assembly shall have a President's Office, consisting of the President, two Vice-Presidents, and a Secretary, elected by the National Assembly when it first meets.

Article 10. The National Assembly in ordinary session shall consider:

(a) The annual report submitted by the Executive Committee on the achievements of the Organisation and its subsidiary bodies.

(b) The annual report of the National Fund and budget allocations.

(c) Proposals submitted by the Executive Committee and recommendations of Assembly committees.

(d) Any other questions submitted to it.

Article 11. The National Assembly shall form such committees as it deems necessary to assist it in the performance of its duties.

These committees shall submit their reports and recommendations to the National Assembly, which shall debate them and issue its decisions as regards them.

Article 12. Attendance by two-thirds of the members of the Assembly shall constitute a quorum. Decisions shall be taken by a majority vote of those present.

CHAPTER III

The Executive Committee

Article 13. (a) All members of the Executive Committee shall be elected by the National Assembly.

(b) The Chairman of the Executive Committee shall be elected by the Committee itself.

(c) The Executive Committee shall be elected from the National Assembly.

Article 14. The Executive Committee shall consist of eleven members, including the Chairman of the Board of Directors of the Palestine National Fund.

Should vacancies occur on the Executive Committee, for any reason, when the National Assembly is not sitting, they shall be filled as follows:

(a) If the vacancies are less than a third of the total membership, they shall not be filled until the first session of the National Assembly.

(b) If the vacancies amount to a third or more of the total membership of the Executive Committee, the National Assembly shall fill them at a session convened for the purpose in not more than thirty days.

(c) Should it be impossible, for valid reasons, to convene the National Assembly in extraordinary session, vacancies arising in either of the above cases shall be filled by the Executive Committee, the Assembly's Bureau and such members of the Assembly as are able to attend, at a joint assembly formed for this purpose. The new members shall be chosen by majority vote of those present.

Article 15. The Executive Committee is the highest executive authority of the Organisation. It shall remain in permanent session, its members devoting themselves exclusively to their work. It shall be responsible for executing the policy, programmes and planning approved by the National Assembly, to which it shall be responsible, collectively and individually.

Article 16. The Executive Committee shall assume responsibility for:

(a) Representing the Palestinian people.

(b) Supervising the Organisation's subsidiary bodies.

(c) Issuing regulations and instructions, and taking decisions on the Organisation's activities, provided these are not incompatible with the Charter or the Constitution.

(d) Implementing the Organisation's financial policy and drafting its budget.

In general, the Executive Committee shall assume all the responsibilities of the Liberation Organisation, in accordance with the general policies and resolutions adopted by the National Assembly.

Article 17. The permanent headquarters of the Executive Committee shall be in Jerusalem. It shall also be entitled to hold its meetings in any other place it sees fit.

Article 18. The Executive Committee shall establish the following departments:

(a) A Military Department.

(b) A Department for Political and Information Affairs.

(c) A Palestine National Fund Department.

(d) A Department for Research and Specialised Institutes.

(e) A Department for Administrative Affairs.

(f) Any other department the Committee considers necessary.

Each department shall have a Director-General and the requisite staff. The authority of each department shall be defined by special regulations drawn up by the Executive Committee.

Article 19. The Executive Committee shall establish close relations and coordinate activities between the Organisation and all Arab and international organisations, federations and institutions which agree with its aims, or which help it in the realisation of the Organisation's objectives.

Article 20. The Executive Committee shall continue to exercise its prerogatives as long as it enjoys the confidence of the National Assembly. The Executive Committee shall submit its resignation to the new National Assembly at its first session. It is subject to re-election.

Article 21. Attendances of two thirds of its members shall constitute a quorum, and its resolutions shall be adopted by majority vote of those present.

CHAPTER IV

General .Rules

Article 22. The Palestine Liberation Organisation shall form an army of Palestinians, to be known as the Palestine Liberation Army, with an independent command which shall operate under the supervision of the Executive Committee, and carry out its instructions and decisions, both general and particular. Its national duty is to become the vanguard in the battle for the liberation of Palestine.

Article 23. The Executive Committee shall make every effort to enroll Palestinians in Arab military colleges and institutes for military training, to mobilise the potentials and resources of the Palestinians, and to prepare them for the battle of liberation.

Article 24. A fund, to be known as the Palestine National Fund, shall be established to finance the activities of the Organisation, which Fund shall be administered by a board of directors to be formed in accordance with special regulations for the Fund issued by the National Assembly.

Article 25. The Fund's sources of revenue shall be:

(a) An impost on Palestinians imposed and collected in accordance with a special system.

(b) Financial assistance provided by Arab governments and the Arab nation.

(c) The sale of "liberation stamps" which the Arab states will issue for use in postal and other transactions.

(d) Contributions and donations.

(e) Arab loans and aid from Arab countries and friendly peoples.

(f) Any other sources of revenue approved by the Assembly.

Article 26. Committees to be known as 'Committees for the Support of Palestine' shall be formed in Arab and friendly countries to collect contributions and support the organisation in its national endeavours.

Article 27. The level at which the Palestinian people is represented in Arab organisations and conferences shall be determined by the Executive Committee. The Executive Committee shall appoint a representative for Palestine to the League of Arab States.

Article 28. The Executive Committee shall be entitled to make such regulations as are necessary for the implementation of the provisions of this constitution.

Article 29. The Organisation's National Assembly shall be empowered to amend, alter, or add to this Constitution by a two thirds majority of its members.

CHAPTER V

Transitional Provisions

Article 30. On July 10, 1968, the National Assembly convened in Cairo shall replace the former Provisional National Assembly of the Palestine Liberation Organisation, and exercise all the prerogatives allotted to it by this Constitution.

Article 31. The National Assembly shall sit for two years as from July 10, 1968. Should it prove impossible to hold elections for its successor, it shall meet and decide either to extend its term for another period or to form a new Assembly in such a manner as it may approve.

Article 32. The National Assembly alone is entitled to co-opt new members from time to time, as it sees fit, should this be desirable in view of the requirements of the battle for liberation and the need to strengthen national unity, in conformity with the provisions of the National Charter, in accordance with regulations to be drafted by the Executive Committee in the coming session.

Appendix D

THE POLITICAL PROGRAM OF THE PALESTINE LIBERATION ORGANIZATION

(January 1973)

Prologue

Throughout its glorious struggle for liberation, democracy and unity, our Arab people has been persistently subject to conspiracies from the colonialist and imperialist forces and their lackey local reactionaries. These colonist and imperialist forces see in our Arab homeland ample opportunity for imperialist plunder of its unlimited natural resources. They regard it, also, as an important strategic take-off point, owing to its unique central position amidst the three continents of Asia, Africa and Europe, and to its control over vital air and sea routes, especially the Mediterranean Sea, the Suez Canal, the Red Sea, the Arabian Gulf and the Indian Ocean. They also view it as a center of gravity for whoever dominates it in international politics.

In their invasion of our Arab homeland, the colonialist and imperialist powers feared that the rising patriotic and national struggle would stand in the way of their schemes. Neither were they confident of the ability of their local reactionary mainstays to hold out against the rising national tide. Hence, using the world Zionist movement, they plotted the usurpation of Palestine, intending to create therein a colonialist racist entity which would constitute both an outpost for the protection of colonialist and Zionist domination over our Arab homeland and a heavy club to be raised by world imperialism in the face of the ever-growing Arab struggle for liberation.

In collusion with the reactionary forces which ruled the whole area—except Syria where a nationalist regime existed—the colonialist and imperialist forces succeeded in planting the colonialist Zionist entity in Palestine arbitrarily and forcibly. They also succeeded in uprooting the Palestinians from their land. The Palestinian Arab people, however, did not submit. On the basis of its right to defend its homeland and its existence, and in view of the responsibility it bears as a forward defense line against the imperialist-Zionist assault on the Arab nation, the Palestinian Arab people, for thirty years, put up a heroic and relentless struggle. In each of its revolutionary uprisings, which culminated in the 1936 and 1947 revolts, the reactionary and lackey forces played a role in undermining the Palestinian struggle and bolstering the position of its enemies and the enemies of the Arab nation.

This was the situation on January 1, 1965, when the vanguard of our Palestinian people initiated the contemporary armed national revolution against the Zionist entity, which exists on Palestinian soil through aggression and the force of arms, and which has never desisted from using violence to expel our people and to finalize the realization of its schemes for the usurpation of the whole of our land. In this revolution, which erupted on that glorious first day of 1965, the vanguard of our people embodied the noble revolutionary traditions of our people and of our Arab nation. They also raised anew the flag of the struggle for liberation against imperialism and Zionism, the flag in whose defense tens of thousands of martyrs have fallen everywhere in the Arab homeland.

This vanguard (with it the Palestinian people, the Arab masses and the free of the world) believed that armed struggle is the correct, the inevitable and the main method of liberating Palestine. For such an antagonistic contradiction with the Zionist enemy cannot be resolved except through revolutionary violence.

When the Palestinian revolutionary vanguard resorted to armed struggle, it aroused the Palestinian and Arab masses, filling them with the will to fight. This led to a violent transformation of Arab realities in the direction of insistence upon rejecting the defeat and determination to take the offensive against the Zionist enemy and to defeat the American imperialist plots. Consequently, Jordan became a base for armed struggle and a take-off point for both the escalation of armed struggle and its protection on Palestinian soil. In addition, extended battle fronts were opened against the enemy which included the Suez Canal and the whole of the Palestinian frontier with Transjordan, Lebanon and Syria. Armed popular resistance was escalated in the West Bank and in the Palestinian terrritory occupied prior to June 1967. The Gaza Strip witnessed heroic deeds of armed struggle to the point where semi-liberated neighbourhoods in Gaza itself were created.

The Palestinian revolution moved from one victory to another and grew quickly, in spite of all the imperialist and Zionist plots and notwithstanding all difficulties. It was able to emerge victorious from all the battles in which it confronted imperialist conspiracies and counter-revolutionary forces in Jordan and Lebanon from November 1968 up to June 1970. The Zionist enemy, too, failed in the extermination campaigns which it conducted against the bases of the revolution. The revolution was able to turn these campaigns of the enemy into victories, as witnessed at Al-Karameh and Al-'Arkoub.

However, the revolution began to face an extremely difficult situation due to the American initiatives and the plans they spawned (such as the Rogers Plan). These initiatives were accompanied by large scale encirclement of the revolution and the spread of the spirit of defeatism. This situation provided the counter-revolutionary forces in Jordan with a valuable opportunity to exploit some of the negative features that characterized the course of the revolution in order to implement the American-Zionist-Hashemite schemes. These schemes aimed at administering a harsh blow to the Palestinian revolution as a preliminary step towards its elimination and towards the liquidation of the Palestine problem. The Palestinian revolution and the Palestinian-Jordanian masses fought gloriously in Jordan in September 1970, in defense of the principle of armed struggle and for the Palestinian and Arab cause. Their battle shall forever remain an epic of incredible heroism and historic resistance under the harshest of conditions. But in July 1971, the lackey Jordanian regime eliminated the public presence of the Palestinian revolution in Jordan and began to follow policies which carried the threat of (a) an official capitulation to the enemy concerning the West Bank and Jerusalem, (b) the liquidation of the unity of the Palestinian presence, (c) the encouragement of dissension among the ranks of the Palestinian people and of divisions between Palestinian and Jordanian, between soldier and fidai, (d) the conversion of the East Bank into a buffer favoring the Zionist entity and into a military, political and economic sphere of influence for Israel, which means transforming it into an American, West German and British backyard where imperialist influence dominates, (e) the repression, pillage and impoverishment of the Jordanian masses, the suppression of their democratic freedoms, in addition to the wrecking of the national economy. It is no secret that the American schemes aim at rebuilding the Jordanian army so it can be directed against Syria and Iraq also. These circumstances presented the Zionist enemy with the golden opportunity for making its occupation more secure by concentrating its efforts on trying to wipe out the armed resistance in the Gaza Strip and pacify the situation in the occupied territories. Thus the Gaza Strip was subjected to the harshest forms of repression and population expulsions; while in the West Bank local municipal elections were imposed to create favorable conditions for the occupation, divide the Palestinian people and attempt at promoting phony political leaders to substitute for the Palestinian revolutionary leadership. This went simultaneously with King Hussein's plan for the establishment of a so-called United Arab Kingdom with goals identical to those of the Zionist plot.

On the other hand, American imperialism intensified its assault according to a broad plan to securely contain and liquidate both the Palestinian revolution and the Arab liberation movement. For this purpose, American imperialism resorted to numerous manoeuvres and plots under such signboards as the so-called American initiatives, peace proposals, interim settlements and United Nations Security Council resolutions. In this they were abetted by active defeatist forces, bound by strong economic and political ties to the imperialists.

The blow that was administered to the Palestinian revolution in Amman in mid-1971, the intensification of the American and Zionist imperialist assault against the Palestinian revolution and the Palestinian masses in the occupied territories and outside, and finally the growing deterioration in the official

Arab situation in favor of capitulation, have all continued to generate a crisis for the Palestinian revolution and the Palestinian and Arab masses. This general crisis has, on the one hand, captivated the whole Arab nation throughout the greater Arab homeland and, on the other, produced a series of conspiratorial schemes aiming at the liquidation of the Palestinian revolution, of the Palestinian people's unified national existence and of its patriotic cause. These conspiracies have taken such forms as the Allon Plan, the proposed Palestinian state on the West Bank and the Gaza Strip, annexation, judaization, as well as the absorption and assimilation of the Palestinians in the societies where they lived in the diaspora.

In this atmosphere of crisis, we find our Palestinian Arab people moving with firmness and determination to defend its armed revolution, its unified national existence and its right to liberate its entire homeland. Our people will allow neither the liquidation of its just cause, nor of its revolution, both of which constitute a central point from which militancy and revolution radiate onto an area over which the imperialists and the Zionists want to extend their full domination.

We also find the constituency of the revolution, its fighters and its mass organizations pushing forcefully and decisively in the direction of national unity, the intensification of armed struggle against the Zionist enemy, the liberation of Jordan, the construction of an Arab front to participate in the struggle with the Palestinian revolution and the establishment of close ties with the world liberation movement and the progressive anti-imperialist forces in the world.

The strong orientation towards national unity among the ranks of the Palestinian revolution does not in itself mean success in overcoming the crisis, but it means creating the necessary conditions for such a step.

Escalating the armed struggle against the Zionist enemy, mobilizing the masses and organizing them, stimulating the various forms of armed and non-armed mass struggle (military, political, economic and cultural), all lead to recapturing the initiative and assuming the offensive, in readiness for over-coming the crisis.

For the Palestinian revolution and for the cause of the

liberation of Palestine, Jordan stands out as something special in comparison to any other Arab country. The Palestinians form a majority in Jordan; this majority has national rights there in addition to its other general rights. It constitutes a principal segment of the Palestinian people without which it is pointless to discuss armed struggle against the enemy. In addition, its struggle has been linked to that of the Transjordanian people and organically linked with contemporary history, especially during the past 25 years. Furthermore the Transjordanian borders with the Zionist enemy are the longest and the closest to its transportation network and to its military, economic and demographic strategic points. From here arise the dangers of the collusion of King Hussein's regime with imperialism and Zionism. This collusion has produced the massacres perpetrated against the Palestinian revolution, the prohibition of its presence in Jordan, the opposition of any activity against either the Zionist enemy or imperialism, and finally the transformation of Jordan into a protective military buffer for the Zionist entity and a route via which Zionist policies and influence in all fields could penetrate. These facts have made the liberation of Jordan (toppling the lackey regime) a decisive factor in overcoming the crisis and a strategic necessity in the process of liberating Palestine.

The creation of an Arab front to participate in the struggle with the Palestinian revolution rests basically upon the belief that no success for our cause is possible except within the framework of a general victory for the national, patriotic and liberating struggle of our Arab nation. This belief will contribute to the protection of the Palestinian revolution, will ensure the continuation and escalation of the armed struggle, will help also in the struggle to topple the lackey regime in Jordan and will generally aid in overcoming the crisis in question.

Strengthening the ties of solidarity and common struggle between the Palestinian revolution and the Arab militant forces on the one hand, and the world liberation movement and the progressive anti-imperialist forces throughout the world on the other, will contribute to the support of our revolutionary struggle and its intensification, as well as to the common struggle of all peoples against imperialism, Zionism, racism and reaction. This strengthening of ties is based on the belief that the Palestinian revolution and the Arab struggle constitute a part of the world struggle for liberation.

In these new and dangerous circumstances and in the face of the responsibilities which the Palestinian revolution bears, the Palestine Liberation Organization, with all its groups and forces, has agreed to an interim political program based on four principal strategic axes:

1. The continuation of the mobilization and organization of all our people's potentials, both within and without the homeland, for a protracted people's war in pursuit of total liberation, and the creation of a democratic state in accordance with the aspirations of the Arab nation for comprehensive unity and national liberation.

2. The tight linking of our people's struggle with that of our brothers the Jordanian people in a Jordanian-Palestinian liberation front to be entrusted (in addition to its tasks in Palestine) with the conduct of the struggle for the liberation of Jordan from the lackey reactionary royalist regime, which acts both to mask actual Zionist domination over the East Bank and to guard fiercely the said Zionist occupation of Palestine.

3. The linking of the Palestinian struggle with the overall Arab struggle *via* a front of all the national and progressive forces hostile to imperialism, Zionism and neo-colonialism.

4. Solidarity with the world struggle against imperialism, Zionism and reaction, and for national liberation.

The Palestine Liberation Organization defines its tasks as follows:

First: On the Palestine Scene

1. To continue the struggle, particularly armed struggle, for the liberation of the entire Palestine national territory and for the establishment of a Palestinian democratic society which guarantees the right to work and to a decent life for all citizens so they can live in equality, justice and fraternity, a democratic society opposed to all forms of prejudice due to race, color or creed.

This society will guarantee the freedoms of thought, expression and assembly, freedom to demonstrate, strike and form national political and labor organizations, freedom of worship for all creeds; such that this democratic Palestinian society will constitute a part of the entire united Arab democratic society.

2. To militate against the compromising mentality and the plans it spawns which are either contrary to our people's cause of national liberation, or aim to liquidate this cause through "proposed Palestinian entities" or through *a Palestinian state on part of the Palestinian national soil.* Also to oppose these plans through armed struggle and political struggle of the masses connected to it.

3. To reinforce the bonds of national unity and joint struggle between our compatriots in the territory occupied in 1948 and those in the West Bank, the Gaza Strip and beyond the occupied homeland.

4. To oppose the policy of clearing the occupied territory of its Arab inhabitants. To confront with violence the erection of colonies and the judaization of parts of the occupied homeland.

5. To mobilize the masses in the West Bank, the Gaza Strip and the entire occupied Palestinian land; also to arm them for the purpose of continuing the struggle and raising their militancy against Zionist settler-colonialism.

6. To direct attention to the organization of our masses in the occupied territory and help mass organizations oppose the Histadrut efforts at drawing Arab workers into its membership. To reinforce and support the Palestinian and Jordanian labor unions' endeavors in realizing the above aim. To oppose the attempts of Zionist political parties at establishing Arab branches in the occupied territory.

7. To support the peasant masses and develop the national economic and cultural institutions in the occupied homeland, in order to strengthen the attachment of citizens there to the land and put an end to the process of emigration. In addition, to oppose the Zionist economic and cultural invasion.

8. To direct attention to the conditions of our citizens in the territory occupied in 1948. To support their struggle for the retention of their Arab national identity. To adopt their problems and help them participate in the struggle for liberation.

9. To direct attention to the welfare of the working masses of our people in the various parts of the Arab homeland by obtaining for them economic and legal rights equal to those of the citizens of Arab societies, considering that their productive potentials are invested in the service of these societies. Particular attention is to be paid to matters pertaining to their right to work, renumerations and compensations, to freedom of political and cultural Palestinian action, and freedom of travel and movement, all this within a frame work preservative of the Palestinian identity.

10. To promote and develop the role of the Palestinian woman, socially, culturally, and economically in the national struggle to seek her participation in all aspects of the struggle.

11. To direct attention to the conditions of our citizens in the camps; to seek to raise their level economically, socially and culturally; to train them in the administration of their own affairs.

12. To encourage workers on Arab farmland and in Arab concerns to remain steadfast in their positions; to undertake to guard them from the lures of employment in enemy projects; to encourage and develop local productivity so as to absorb workers employed by the enemy; to oppose enemy attempts at taking over national productive enterprises and ruining them.

13. To consider every collaborator, or person negligent of the historic natural right of the Palestinian people in their homeland, a target of the revolution, be it in his person or his possessions. So, too, every conspirator against any of our people's rights, primarily its right to oppose the occupation and its right to national independence.

14. To direct attention to our emigrant masses in foreign countries and to act to link them to their cause and to the Palestinian revolution.

15. The Palestine Liberation Organization shall use its official Arab relations for the protection of the Palestinian citizens' interests in the Arab homeland and for the expression of the Palestinian people's political will. (The Palestinian revolution shall continue to represent the legitimate political leadership of the Palestinian people and to be its sole spokesman in all fateful matters.) Hence the organs of leadership of the Palestine Liberation Organization shall be formed from all the organizations of the armed Palestinian revolution, the organizations of the Palestinian masses (trade-union and cultural organizations) and from patriotic groups and personalities who uphold armed struggle as a principal and fundamental means for the liberation of Palestine and are committed to the Palestinian National Charter.

Second: On the Jordanian-Palestinian Scene

The Jordanian-Palestinian national front is called upon to direct the struggle of the two peoples towards the following strategic aims:

(A) The establishment of a national democratic regime in Jordan which shall:

Create the appropriate atmosphere for the continuation of the struggle for the liberation of the whole of Palestine;

Guarantee the national sovereignty of both Jordanian and Palestinian peoples;

Guarantee the renewal of the union of the two banks on the correct basis of the complete national equality between the two peoples, so that the full historical national rights of the Palestinian people and the present national rights of the two peoples are safeguarded;

Ensure common national development economically, socially and culturally;

Strengthen the ties of brotherhood and equality between the two peoples by means of equal legal, constitutional, cultural and economic rights and by means of placing the human and economic resources of each people in the service of their common development.

(B) The consolidation of the struggles of both the

Palestinian and Jordanian peoples with that of the Arab nation so as to:

Complete national liberation;

Oppose imperialist plans aiming at imposing solutions and conditions in the Arab homeland that mean surrender to the enemy;

Eradicate all forms of Zionist and imperialist presence (economic, military and cultural), as well as all the forces connected with them which act as mediators for neo-colonialism and its policies.

In order for this Jordanian-Palestinian national front to actually emerge on the Jordanian scene, and to grow and gain strength, all forms of day-to-day mass struggle must be immediately activated, so that the agitation of the masses for both their daily and general demands leads to the rise of an organized leadership and organizations expressive of the interests of the various segments of the masses, i.e. the kind of leadership and organizations that have been absent from the day-to-day fights of the masses over the past years.

The realization of the general goals of the Palestinian-Jordanian national front requires a long and hard struggle. Through day-to-day struggles and partial battles, the masses surmount all social obstacles of a parochial nature and fuse in common struggle showing their militant national features and exposing the lackey royalist regime. The royalist regime depends fundamentally upon the exploitation of tribal relations and upon the provocation of parochial fanaticism in order to hide its collaboration with Zionism and imperialism (also to divert the attention of the masses from their contradiction with the regime.) The Palestine Liberation Organization presents the program of action for Jordan to engage the militant organizations in Jordan in a serious fraternal debate with the purpose of building the Palestinian-Jordanian national front. This front must apply itself to the following tasks:

1. Mobilizing and organizing the masses for the establishment of a national democratic regime in Jordan which believes in the Palestinian revolution, supports it and provides the climate necessary for all modes of mass struggle.

2. Bringing the Jordanians to participate in the armed struggle against the Zionist enemy inasmuch as this is a patriotic and national goal as well as a necessity for the protection of the East Bank of Jordan.

3. Struggling:

to establish the Palestinian revolution's freedom of action in and from Jordan and the formation of bases on its soil,

to expose the conspiracies of the lackey regime and its falsehoods in this respect,

to ensure mass protection of the fighters moving off westwards beyond the river.

4. Acting to consolidate the national and anti-imperialist forces throughout the Arab homeland in one militant front and to deepen militant ties between the Palestinian-Jordanian national struggle and the world revolutionary forces.

Third: Relations with the Arab Revolutionary Forces

The Arab revolution is now passing through the phase of implementing the democratic national revolution which militates:

(A) To realize complete political and economic independence and eradicate all forms of division and dependence upon colonialism and imperialism.

(B) To liquidate all forms of imperialist presence such as political influence, military bases, economic investments, cultural institutions, and the defeat of all the local forces connected with it.

(C) To liberate Palestine from the Zionist-imperialist entity which not only usurped the Palestinian land and expelled its indigenous population, but has also proved to be, throughout its existence, a main imperialist tool for undermining the Arab revolution and protecting the imperialist presence in the area. The liberation of Palestine is not only a Palestinian patriotic duty. It is also a national necessity. The struggle for the realization of the Arab national democratic revolution will be neither unified nor deepened, nor will it broaden and succeed in achieving its purposes, except by liquidating the Zionist imperialist base which aims at its very foundations.

(D) To safeguard the freedom of the Arab masses so they can exercise their role in political life and constitute a solid basis for a firmly established democratic Arab unity.

(E) To place the material and human resources of the Arab nation at the service of economic, social and cultural development with the purpose of reinforcing political and economic independence, realizing Arab economic and cultural integration and eradicating all forms of backwardness and division.

The unity of the Palestinian revolution and the Palestinian-Jordanian national struggle constitutes an integral part of the Arab democratic national revolution and one of its main axes.

Hence, the task of the Palestinian revolution, and its leadership, and that of the Jordanian national front is:

To seek to join with all the militant Arab national democratic organizations wherever they exist;

To prepare, though struggle, a militant atmosphere conducive to the rise of such forces;

To open its ranks to Arab militants, for the struggle in the Palestinian arena against the imperialist Zionist enemy is a main strategic struggle of the entire Arab revolution.

The Arab progressive national forces must combine in an Arab national front with the following demands: ,

1. To reinforce the positive support of the Palestinian national revolution and of the Jordanian-Palestinian national democratic struggle.

2. To struggle against all liquidationist plans or interim settlements, not only because they consecrate Zionist usurpation and lead to the elimination of the Palestinian national cause, but also because they have proved to be preparations for imperialist and allied reactionary manoeuvres and conspiracies for tearing asunder the unity of the Arab national forces, for eradicating the Arab national revolution and for imposing complete imperialist domination over the area.

3. To struggle for the elimination of the present forms of imperialist presence in the Arab homeland (political influence, military bases, investments and cultural institutions and activities). To struggle against the domination of an imperialist economy over the Arab national economy. To struggle against the reactionary forces which propagandize for this domination and stimulate it. The continuation of American interests in the Arab homeland and their organic relations requires the confrontation and liquidation of these American-imperialist interests.

4. To encourage and support all institutions and activities which (a) seek to revive or protect the Arab national heritage; (b) diffuse national and revolutionary values and virtues; (c) undertake the task of opposing the Zionist-imperialist cultural invasion and the decadent and base values it propagates.

5. Solidarity with Arab patriotic and progressive militants against any persecution which touches their means of livelihood or touches them either physically, politically or intellectually.

Fourth: Relation with the Forces of Liberation in the World

The Palestinian national struggle and the Arab national democratic struggle are an integral part of the militant movement against imperialism and racism and for national liberation throughout the world. Mutual solidarity and support between the Arab national struggle and the world revolutionary struggle are a necessity and an objective condition for the success of our Arab struggle.

The Arab national and progressive forces base the ties of world solidarity on the following principles:

1. The Arab Palestinian national struggle is decisively and firmly on the side of the unity of all world revolutionary forces.

2. The contribution of the Arab national struggle towards resolving any disagreements within the world revolutionary movement consists in its effective and successful treatment of its own problems and the challenges which it faces.

3. The goals and methods of the Arab struggle, (which take account of the general rules of revolution which, in turn, are the gist of the experiences of the world national liberation movements) concern the Arab national and progressive forces. This does not mean neglect or disregard of the observations and advice of friends.

Appendix E

Political Programme for the Present Stage of the Palestine Liberation Organization Drawn up by the Palestinian National Council, Cairo, June 9, 1974.[1]

The Palestinian National Council:

On the basis of the Palestinian National Charter and the Political Programme drawn up at the Eleventh Session, held from January 6–12, 1973; and from its belief that it is impossible for a permanent and just peace to be established in the area unless our Palestinian people recover all their national rights and, first and foremost, their rights to return and to self-determination on the whole of the soil of their homeland; and in the light of a study of the new political circumstances that have come into existence in the period between the Council's last and present sessions, resolves the following:

1. To reaffirm the Palestine Liberation Organization's previous attitude to Resolution 242, which obliterates the national right of our people and deals with the cause of our people as a problem of refugees. The Council therefore refuses to have anything to do with this resolution at any level, Arab or international, including the Geneva Conference.

2. The Liberation Organization will employ all means, and first and foremost armed struggle, to liberate Palestinian territory and to establish the independent combatant national authority for the people over every part of Palestinian territory that is liberated. This will require further changes being effected in the balance of power in favour of our people and their struggle.

3. The Liberation Organization will struggle against any proposal for a Palestinian entity the price of which is recognition, peace, secure frontiers, renunciation of national rights

1. Published in Wafa (Beirut), June 9, 1974.

147

and the deprival of our people of their right to return and their right to self-determination on the soil of their homeland.

4. Any step taken towards liberation is a step towards the realization of the Liberation Organization's strategy of establishing the democratic Palestinian state specified in the resolutions of previous Palestinian National Councils.

5. Struggle along with the Jordanian national forces to establish a Jordanian-Palestinian national front whose aim will be to set up in Jordan a democratic national authority in close contact with the Palestinian entity that is established through the struggle.

6. The Liberation Organization will struggle to establish unity in struggle between the two peoples and between all the forces of the Arab liberation movement that are in agreement on this programme.

7. In the light of this programme, the Liberation Organization will struggle to strengthen national unity and to raise it to the level where it will be able to perform its national duties and tasks

8. Once it is established, the Palestinian national authority will strive to achieve a union of the confrontation countries, with the aim of completing the liberation of all Palestinian territory, and as a step along the road to comprehensive Arab unity.

9. The Liberation Organization will strive to strengthen its solidarity with the socialist countries, and with forces of liberation and progress throughout the world, with the aim of frustrating all the schemes of Zionism, reaction and imperialism.

10. In the light of this programme the leadership of the revolution will determine the tactics which will serve and make possible the realization of these objectives.

The Executive Committee of the Palestine Liberation Organization will make every effort to implement this programme, and should a situation arise affecting the destiny and the future of the Palestinian people, the National Assembly will be convened in extraordinary session.

Appendix F

The Political Resolutions of the 13th Palestine National Council

with commentaries by Y. Harkabi

There has never been a session of the Palestine National Council (PNC) whose resolutions were so eagerly awaited in many circles as the last one which convened in Cairo from March 12 to 20, 1977. The resolutions concluded by this council were the result of a bargaining and compromise process on the part of the various Palestine groups. Nevertheless, as has always been the case at the previous PNCs, the mainstream of the PLO prevailed. The opposition, represented by the Rejection Front, gained a few marginal concessions to its demands from the majority which conceded in order to preserve unity. Significantly, in the final vote, against a majority of *194* which voted for the resolutions, only a tiny faction of 13 members of the PFLP voted against the resolutions, whereas Rejection Fedayeen groups such as the 'Arab Liberation Front' and the 'PFLP-General Command' supported the resolutions and even joined the new PLO Executive Committee set up by the 13th PNC to implement its resolutions.

The majority of the Rejection Front yielded on two fundamental issues: the establishment of the West Bank Palestine State and the participation of the PLO in international conferences dealing with the Arab-Israeli conflict. It had previously rejected both vehemently. Its acceptance of such steps is conditional on their not entailing a recognition of Israel or peace, i.e., that the road to irredentism will stay wide open. Such conditions raised no difficulty as they represent the view of the mainstream as well.

The Rejection Front criticized the PLO establishment for its submissiveness to the Syrians in the Lebanese war and its readiness to negotiate with Jordan. Under such criticism the majority gave way and waived an article calling for negotiations with Jordan. In return, the traditional call for the overturn of the Hashemite regime, which has been repeated in PNC resolutions of recent years, was dropped.

The present resolutions express the views of the mainstream composing the majority in the PLO and which is mistakenly referred to as 'moderate.' The extremeness of the resolutions demonstrates the inherent difficulties of moderating the PLO position, even tactically, despite Arab governments' pleas and pressures. This resilience stems from the absolutism and totalism which characterize the PLO position of laying claim to Palestine in its *entirety*. Hence, moderating its position implies the relinquishment of PLO's central idea or the core-value of its ideology. The cohesiveness of this ideology as one integral system renders a partial incremental or gradual change difficult.

Had the extremists won in this Council, one could entertain a hope that in the next round the 'moderates' might have their way and change the resolutions. But as it was the moderates who adopted the extreme resolutions, hope for moderating the PLO position is diminished.

There is nothing significantly new in the resolutions. The thinking of the PLO has long ago crystallized and congealed. Their claim to participate in conferences dealing with the Arab-Israeli conflict may *prima facie* seem new. However, the conditions attached to this participation, namely, that it would not be based on Resolution 242 and that no peace and recognition would be the outcome of such a conference (Article 9), are a contradiction in terms—a settlement without a settlement. The expectation of the PLO position and of some Arab quarters that Israel withdraw while leaving all doors open to the Arabs to pursue their multiform struggle against it, is indeed the height of political perversity.

The text of the resolutions with annotations follows:

Preamble:

The National Palestine Council proceeding from the Palestine National Charter and the previous National Council resolutions; considering the decisions and political gains achieved by the

PLO at the Arab international levels during the period following the 12th session of the PNC; after studying and debating the latest developments in the Palestine issue; and stressing support for the Palestine national struggle in the Arab and international forums, affirms the following:

Had the Covenant or Charter been an onerous burden of which the PLO wished to rid itself, the PNC could have refrained from referring to it, for consigning a revered ideological document to oblivion can serve as a means of *de facto* abrogating it. Here, on the contrary, the PNC categorically declares its allegiance to the Covenant and to the resolutions of the previous PNCs, as a source for its own resolutions. Thus the authority of the Covenant is reconfirmed as are the Ten Points of the last PNC (the 12th).

Reverent references to the Covenant are not mandatory in PNC resolutions. They did not occur in the resolutions of the 2nd and 3rd PNCs in Shuqairy's days. In the ensuing period after Shuqairy's demise the PLO became a coalition of Fedayeen organizations disputing and competing amongst themselves. The Covenant acquired functional importance, providing a common denominator which linked them together and assured the coherence of the movement. The reference to the Covenant in the preamble is important, as a deliberate rebuttal of the prognostications from various sources that it would be changed as a result of demands addressed to the Council to amend it. The frequency of references to the Covenant by Palestinian spokesmen has greatly increased in the last months which also bears evidence of the vitality of this document. Such references are repeated in the other resolutions of the 13th PNC.

Article 1. **The PNC affirms that the Palestine issue is the essence and the root of the Arab-Zionist conflict. Security Council Resolution 242 ignores the Palestinian people and their firm rights. The PNC therefore confirms its rejection of this resolution, and rejects negotiations at the Arab and international levels based on this resolution.**

The 4th PNC (July 1968) rejected Security Council Resolution 242 for a host of reasons, first and foremost because of its stipulation of recognition and a settlement of the conflict including secure and recognized borders. Here one main fault in Resolution 242 is brandished, i.e. its ignoring the firm or inalienable rights of the Palestinian people, which in the PLO conception imply its rights to the entire territory of Palestine. Thus such an inalienable right may imply an indirect, euphemistic expression for the liquidation of Israel. The inalienable rights (in Arabic *'thabita'*—permanent) is presumably identical to the 'historical rights' in Sadat's nomenclature in his opening speech of the Popular Congress and 10th PNC which he differentiated from the more, it seems, restrictive right which he termed the 'present' (*rāhina*) to a small Palestinian state. Hence Resolution 242 is rejected as it is incompatible with the demand for the demise of Israel. Article 1 in the resolution follows a similar article in the 12th PNC's resolution, except for the omission of an explicit reference to a rejection of the Geneva conference.

The conflict is referred to as 'Arab-Zionist' rather than as Arab-Israeli, its usual name. Such an appellation falls within a tendency in PLO parlance to shun the mention of 'Israelis', calling them Jews, as any acknowledgement that Israelis exist implies that they have some collective quality besides their religion and that they are, at least, a nation in the making, contradicting the PLO's basic conception that the Jews constitute a religion only. In Arab political literature, the opposition to Zionism is much greater than that to Israel as a state. The depravity of Israel flows from its being, first and foremost, the creation of Zionism. Zionism is defined as Jewish nationalism, which is an aberration, as the Jews are not a nation. Thus, describing the conflict as between a normal group—the Arabs—and a depraved movement such as Zionism which has been internationally condemned predisposes the judgement in favour of the Arabs.

Article 2. **The PNC affirms the stand of the PLO and its determination to continue the armed struggle, and its concomitant form of political and mass struggle to achieve our inalienable national rights.**

PLO resolutions have repeatedly stipulated that the

armed struggle is the main form of struggle and that other forms are secondary and ancillary. The 'mass struggle,' which is added here, refers to protests and civil disobedience in the occupied territories. The importance of such activities has recently been given greater prominence in the PLO arsenal as other venues of action from Jordan, Syria and Lebanon have been closed to them. The importance of this issue is reflected in the fact that another article is allotted to it.

Article 3. **The PNC affirms that the struggle, in all its military, political and popular forms, in the occupied territories, constitutes the central link in its program of struggle. On this basis, the PLO will strive to escalate the armed struggle in the occupied territory, to escalate all other concomitant forms of struggle, and to give all kinds of moral support to the masses of our people in the occupied territory in order to escalate the struggle and to strengthen their steadfastness to defeat and liquidate the occupation.**

The passing of the onus of struggle to the population of the occupied territories calls for expression of support and sympathy towards it. 'The occupied territory' can refer also to Israel within the green lines as was its common appelation in Arab political parlance.

Article 4. **The PNC affirms the PLO's stand which rejects all types of American capitulationist settlement and all liquidationist projects. The Council affirms the determination of the PLO to abort any settlement achieved at the expanse of the firm national rights of our people. The PNC calls upon the Arab nation to shoulder its pan-Arab responsibilities and to pool all its energies to confront these imperialist and Zionist plans.**

'Liquidationist projects' refer to plans for the settlement of the conflict through compromise, without a full realization of the PLO demands for the whole of Palestine (see Article 21 of the Covenant). Any compromise is condemned as 'surrender,' thus stigmatizing it both intellectually and emotionally. The 'liquidation of the Palestine problem' and the 'liquidation of

Israel' are juxtaposed as mutually exclusive and exhaustive alternatives. Insuring the existence of Israel in any size is tantamount to the liquidation of the Palestinian problem. Such statements of position depict PLO absolutism which does not recognize partial satisfaction of its claims.

Article 5. **The Palestine National Council stresses the importance and necessity of national unity, both political and military, among the contingents of the Palestine revolution within the framework of the PLO, because this is one of the basic conditions for victory. For this reason, it is necessary to coordinate national unity on the basis of commitment to all these resolutions, and to draw up programs which will ensure the implementation of this.**

This is an organizational article calling for unity. Similar articles have been common in PLO resolutions. The weakening of various organizations may facilitate steps toward unification, or at least their coming closer together as the spectrum of views which separated them has recently narrowed.

Article 6. **The PNC affirms the right of the Palestine revolution to be present on the soil of fraternal Lebanon within the framework of the Cairo Agreement and its appendices, concluded between the PLO and the Lebanese authorities. The Council also affirms adherence to the implementation of the Cairo Agreement in letter and in spirit, including the preservation of the position of the revolution and the security of the camps. The PNC refuses to accept any interpretation of this agreement by one side only. Meanwhile, it affirms its eagerness for the maintenance of the sovereignty and security of Lebanon.**

The 'Palestine Revolution' is an honorific term for the Palestinian struggle against Israel. The right to continue the incursions into Israel and the right to operate in Lebanon should be preserved, against developments within Lebanon, including the Syrian take-over which may further restrict PLO freedom of action. This article embodies two contradictory elements: Lebanese sovereignty and Palestinian freedom of action. However, as demonstrated through experience, the latter infringes upon the former.

The PLO invokes the agreement with Lebanon of November 3, 1969 which allowed Palestinian action from Lebanon albeit within limitations which were specified in it and in its annexes (protocols). Rejection of a 'unilateral interpretation' of the Cairo agreement refers to discussions of the Arab League 'Quadripartite Commission' on imposing restrictive regulations of the PLO in Lebanon.

Article 7. **The PNC greets the heroic fraternal Lebanese people and affirms the eagerness of the PLO for the maintenance of the territorial integrity of Lebanon, the unity of its people and its security, independence, sovereignty and Arabism. The PNC affirms its pride in the support rendered by this heroic fraternal people to the PLO, which is struggling for our people to regain their national rights to their homeland and their right to return to this homeland. The PNC strongly affirms the need to deepen and consolidate cohesion between all Lebanese nationalist forces and the Palestine revolution.**

Lebanese support of the Palestinians in the previous article is complemented by support of the Palestinians for Lebanese sovereignty etc., which in practice, fell short of the commitment as expressed in this article. The 'Nationalist forces' probably refer to the leftist as the others are branded as 'isolationists.' Preserving Lebanon's integrity implies opposition to participation and moreover an assurance that the Palestinians do not aspire to take a region in Lebanon for themselves as an 'alternative homeland,' as some Lebanese circles have accused them.

Supporting Lebanese Arabism means, as well, opposition to changing Lebanese unitary structure since partition into a Muslim and Christian region implies that communalism is stronger than a unitary bond of Arab nationalism.

Article 8. **The Council affirms the need to strengthen the Arab Front participating in the Palestine revolution, and to deepen cohesion with all forces participating in it in all Arab countries, as well as to escalate the joint Arab struggle and to further strengthen the Palestine revolution in order to contend with the imperialist and Zionist designs.**

The 'Participating Front' is a framework of organizations and parties organized in order to support the PLO by exerting pressure on Arab governments to prevent them from action against the PLO. The need for such an organization was a lesson learned from the PLO débâcle in Jordan in 1970–1. Once established, Kamal Junblat headed it. Organizing such a front meant intervention in the internal affairs of Arab states. The Lebanese catastrophe does not discourage the PLO from continuing the same policy. The 'Participating Front' was originally established for internal purposes. However, this article implies its use in the field of external affairs —as a bulwark against foreign pressures.

Article 9. **The PNC has decided to consolidate Arab struggle and solidarity on the basis of struggle against imperialism and Zionism, to work for the liberation of all occupied Arab areas, and to adhere to the support for the Palestine revolution in order to regain the constant national rights of the Arab Palestinian people without any conciliation (*sulh*—peace) or recognition (of Israel).**

The need to strengthen Arab solidarity is a recurring theme at Arab meetings. The solidarity described here is not rooted positively in a social and ideological common approach, but negatively in participation in the struggle against external foreign forces.

The second half of this article states that whatever the political settlement may be, recognition of Israel and peace with it are categorically proscribed.

Article 10. **The PNC affirms the right of the PLO to exercise its struggle responsibilities at the pan-Arab level and through any Arab land in the interest of liberating the occupied areas.**

Hence the PLO's right to operate in any Arab country and through it against Israel. This claim is directed now in the main toward Jordan, but also toward Syria and Lebanon. The PLO has the right to act in the international arena, i.e., mainly the U.N.

This article stipulates that the PLO's responsibility is not limited to the Palestinian (*watanī*) domain but extends to the pan-Arab (*qawmī*) one. Presumably such a line is based on the Rabat Summit Meeting resolution of 29 October, 1974 which authorized the PLO to lay down the general Arab line of policy in the conflict, to which all Arab states undertook a solemn obligation to adhere.

Article 11. **The PNC has decided to continue to struggle to regain the national rights of our people, in particular their rights of return, self-determination and establishing an independent national state on their national soil.**

In the 12th PNC, the state in the West Bank was called 'an authority,' so calling it a 'state' is not a major change though it does signify greater acceptance of such a state.

The merit of this article is its ambiguity. Internally it may be understood as applying to Palestine in its entirety, as the traditional PLO objective calls for. Externally it may be interpreted as referring to a small Palestinian state. Foreign protagonists of the PLO may make use of the second version, as a proof of PLO moderation. What the true intention of these two versions is can be learned from the tenor of the whole resolution and from the Political Statement published by the Council accompanying its resolutions in which the objective of setting up the Palestinian Democratic State is explicitly stated. The right to return includes the right to get back all former Arab landed property, the return of which will cause the mass eviction of Israelis from Jaffa, Nazareth, Ramle, etc. 'The return' is thus both a strategic objective and a principle in the Palestinian program of action leading toward the demise of Israel. From juxtaposing this article with Article 9 it can be concluded that the setting up of a Palestinian state is not a final settlement of the conflict, as it will not entail peace and recognition.

Article 12. **The PNC affirms the significance of cooperation and solidarity with socialist, non-aligned Islamic and African countries, and with all the national liberation movements in the world.**

Ever since its inception, the PLO has expressed orientation toward the Eastern Bloc and the developing countries.

Article 13. **The PNC hails the stands and struggles of all the democratic countries and forces against Zionism in its capacity as one form of racism, as well as against its aggressive practices.**

The Council thanks all nations who supported the General Assembly November 10, 1975 resolution condemning Zionism, thus undermining the ideological foundation on which Israel as a state was established.

Article 14. **The PNC affirms the significance of establishing relations and coordination with the progressive and democratic Jewish forces inside and outside the occupied homeland, since these forces are struggling against Zionism as a doctrine and in practice. The PNC calls on all states and forces who love freedom, justice and peace in the world to end all forms of assistance and cooperation with the racist Zionist regime, and to end contacts with it and its instruments.**

The circles with which some PLO personalities have had contacts are specified as anti-Zionist as demanded by the PLO circles who opposed such contacts. The connection between progressiveness, support of the PLO and anti-Zionism seems to be understood as inherent. Zionism in Arab political thinking is described as Jewish nationalism. Anti-Zionism means opposition to the establishment of a Jewish state and advocating its dismantlement now that it exists. Thus the purpose of anti-Zionism is to eradicate the Zionist character of Israel. The uniqueness of Israel as a Jewish state will fade out and it will become like all other countries in the region and dissolve in it, i.e., cease to exist.

Article 15. **Taking into consideration the important achievements in the Arab and international arenas since the conclusion of the PNC's 12th session, the Palestine National Council, which has reviewed the political report submitted by the PLO, has decided on the following:**

A. The Council confirms its wish for the PLO's rights to participate independently and on an equal footing in all the conferences and international forums concerned with the Palestine issue and the Arab-Zionist conflict, with a view to achieving our inalienable national rights as approved by the UN General Assembly in 1974, namely in Resolution 3236.

B. The Council declares that any settlement or agreement affecting the rights of our Palestinian people made in the absence of this people will be completely null and void.

This is perhaps the most important operative article. The PLO claims the right to participate in any international conference, first and foremost, presumably, Geneva, although this is not mentioned explicitly. Such participation would be on the basis of the General Assembly resolution of November 22, 1974, which granted the PLO international recognition and status and stated that 'the Palestinian people are indispensable for the solution of the question of Palestine,' and 'a principal party in the establishment of a just and durable peace in the Middle East.' Using this resolution, the Council tries to circumvent Resolution 242 which constitutes the basis for the Geneva conference.

The second part of the article is directed against the Arab states, threatening rejection of any settlement achieved without the participation of the PLO. Thus, the Arab states had better refrain from any conference from which the PLO is excluded. The PLO claims veto power over a settlement concerning the Palestinian problem. Such a resolution presents a challenge to a state like Egypt. Thus, Egypt presses emphatically for PLO participation in the Geneva conference, irrespective of its rejection of Resolution 242.

DISCARD

BETHADY
COLLEGE
LIBRARY